AF574330

A Practical Approach for
Director, Actor & Designer

A Practical Approach for Director, Actor & Designer

edited by Robert Smyth

World Wide Publications
A ministry of the Billy Graham Evangelistic Association
1303 Hennepin Avenue,
Minneapolis, Minnesota 55403

DEVELOPING A DRAMA GROUP
A Practical Approach for Director, Actor & Designer

World Wide Publications is the publishing ministry of the Billy Graham Evangelistic Association.

Photo credits: all photos by Nathan R. Peirson, except pages 41 (rt. & bot.), 52, 129 and 134 by Christian Turner; page 58 by Robert Smyth; and pages 54, 60, and 71 by Dave Ward.

Illustrations by Timothy L. Pagaard.

Library of Congress Catalog Card Number: 89-051182

ISBN: 0-89066-185-5

Printed in the United States of America

To Steve Terrell
—actor, director, teacher, visionary—
whose energy for the theater and dedication to his Lord
laid the foundation for Lamb's Players

Contents

Introduction

One day last year some of us happened to notice a file box bulging in the corner of our office. Were we imagining things, or had the box grown? But we were late for rehearsal and had no time to investigate. We forgot about the box, and over the next months it continued to swell unattended. Then one day during a staff meeting, we heard it. The box, filled beyond capacity, had groaned. We could ignore it no longer. Someone suggested—"Perhaps we really should do something with all that unanswered mail." So, mustering our corporate courage, we approached the box. Gingerly we opened it. It shuddered, and out poured a torrent of notes, letters, and phone messages, each with its separate plea:

"Should Christians be involved in theater?"

"Where can I get scripts?"

"How do we start a drama group?"

"Is it possible to do this and keep my sanity?"

"I've just been put in charge of a drama program."

"Please help!!!"

Looking at each other and at the pile before us, we decided it was time to roll up our sleeves and go to work. It was time to be responsible—to answer our mail. It was time to . . . write a book!

Piece of cake, we thought. After all, we were big boys and girls. As a company, Lamb's Players had been around for over eighteen years. Our ensemble had worked in a wide variety of theater forms—evangelistic street theater, drama for the church, a professional resident theater, puppetry, mime, and dance. We'd had a good track record. We'd just squeeze the book out between rehearsals, performances, production meetings, and all the other things we juggled to keep Lamb's Players going. Why, this would be easy, fun, and exciting.

Exciting it has been. Fun? In some ways. Easy? No! We're hands-on artists here—actors, directors, designers, technicians, and even a playwright or two. But writing a "how to" book was something new.

It soon demanded the labor of everyone on our small staff. A lot of overtime was given to it, and a lot of prayer. It has been a challenge to put theatrical knowledge and experience into clear, practical, written form—all the while keeping the gears running smoothly on a full-time, year-round production schedule.

But *Developing a Drama Group* has proven to be a labor of love—love for this amazing art form to which each of us feels called, and love for our imaginative Creator, the giver of all good gifts.

Although we wrote the book with an eye toward developing a drama group within a church, much of the information and ideas here are applicable to someone developing a drama program in a school, a community theater, or with a nonprofit touring company. We hope you'll be helped by the book's practical suggestions and inspired to add your own ideas to this introductory foundation.

There are some things *Developing a Drama Group* is not. It is not a book of scripts. If that's what you're after we have two suggestions: (1) search the "Resources" section beginning on page 241, where you'll find a good list of publishers and production companies that offer scripts, and (2) ask for our book, *Lamb's Players Presents 15 Surefire*

Scripts, also published by World Wide Publications.

Another thing *Developing a Drama Group* is not—it is not the last word on drama. For some it will be a good introduction. For others, a handy reference. There are many fine books out there that go into greater detail on each of the specific areas we cover. You will find a useful list of books in the section entitled "Further Reading," beginning on page 255.

Finally, this book does not pretend to be an analytical, theoretical, or apologetic treatise on the theater. We don't spend time trying to justify a Christian's involvement in the dramatic arts. That battle has been fought in other arenas. We may throw out an occasional thought or opinion here and there, but we're primarily working artists, not scholars or teachers.

A quick note about our use of gender. In writing the book, we chose to avoid the awkward *he/she* form by simply alternating the use of *he* and *she* . We use *actor* as a non-gender word, like *doctor.* You might also notice that we do not use the terms *Christian drama.* You'll find an explanation for this in chapter 12, "A Wider View."

1
Drama and the Church

There is no creativity without faith and hope.
—Thornton Wilder

Everywhere you look these days it seems another church has "discovered" drama. And that's a little ironic, because that is where it all began. After a four hundred year absence from Western culture, the theater experienced revival in the tenth century A.D. and this rebirth took place in the church. The first actors were clergy; the first scripts were Scripture. Someone had the idea to act out a story from the Bible. Soon, what began as a simple Easter production spread throughout the church year. The church found that drama was a powerful means of communication. The enacting of events and lessons from the Bible made them memorable because they were understood on an emotional level. Congregations swelled when drama was presented. It became an important aid to teaching and worship.

With time these dramas moved beyond the borders of the church. The trade guilds began producing plays. Troupes of traveling actors sprang up across Europe. As theater began to reflect more secular themes, scripts often became coarse, lewd, and cynical. In reaction to this, the church eventually condemned the theater outside its walls and rejected the use of drama inside. While some art forms continued to flourish in the church—poets and musicians found expression in prayers and hymns, and visual artists and architects contributed substantially—the dramatic arts were kept outside. As the center of Western culture moved further and further from its Christian foundation, the church also began to retreat more and more from the surrounding culture.

Not only did the church lose its leadership and influence in the arts outside its walls, but it began to regard *all* the arts with a growing suspicion. For almost two hundred years its artistic expression has been limited to traditional forms of music and visual arts that are safe and familiar; and likewise, the salt of Christianity has been regrettably absent from the theater.

But now, slowly, things are coming full circle. The twentieth-century church is beginning to rediscover the dramatic arts. It is hard to pinpoint just exactly how or when this renewal began, but somewhere around the late 1920s in England and the mid 1930s in the United States, large-scale dramatic presentations began to find their way back into some churches. By the 1950s a number of large denominations were encouraging drama programs in their churches.

The clergy in the Middle Ages saw the impact of drama when they enacted events from the Bible.

Liturgical churches, with their historic understanding of the power of dramatic symbols, produced chancel dramas in sanctuaries across the country.

The Jesus Movement of the late 1960s brought with it new excursions into the arts. Old forms were discarded as fresh expressions celebrated the believer's life in Christ. Though often rough and naive, this music, poetry, and drama had an urgency and life in it. A freer expression in dramatic forms was also encouraged in the black church. Many black performing artists working on Broadway today trace their start in music and drama to their churches.

During the 1970s and early 1980s, Dr. Francis Schaeffer had a tremendous influence in opening up the evangelical church to the arts. Many young Christians were encouraged to pursue the arts as a valid vocation. In ways that we have not yet fully recognized, much of the current explosion of professional activity by Christians in the arts stems from Schaeffer's work.

The church today is exploring fresh ways to communicate to the society around it. Many churches recognize that while the truth of Scripture does not change, cultural expression does. We are a nation accustomed to the dramatic form. From bedtime stories and school plays to TV and movies, we have been raised on dramatic communication.

Today, the church is experiencing a surge of activity in the dramatic arts. Christians are now producing theater both within the church walls and outside them. In the English-speaking world, the United Kingdom has set a great example. Church drama groups, performing arts festivals, celebration evangelism (where drama plays a large part), professional touring theater companies, and artist support groups have all flourished.

In the United States and Canada many churches now have drama groups that perform every week as part of the worship service. The drama group has become part of the model for many church growth programs.

Professional and amateur touring companies are on the road year-round. Whether part of a larger para-church organization like Youth With a Mission, or a professional drama company like the Refreshment Committee in Minneapolis, these groups present a variety of dramatic presentations in churches, schools, hospitals, prisons, military bases, and even on street corners.

Artist fellowships, often patterned after London's Arts Center Group, are popping up in major cities across the country. National support groups, like Christians In Theatre Arts and the Director's Alliance, and communication networks like CAN (Christians in the Arts Networking), encourage the development of a Christian voice in the dramatic arts.

Professional resident theater companies like Lamb's Players in San Diego, Acacia Theatre in Milwaukee, Pacific Theatre in Vancouver, AD Players in Houston, and Taproot Theatre in Seattle, are producing work reflecting a Christian worldview and striving for high artistic standards.

All of this is to say that you are in good company! Exciting things are happening. Come along in this adventure, as the church reclaims the arts. In them and through them, let us give glory to our creative Lord!

2
Starting Up

So you want to start a drama group. You're energetic. You see great opportunities out there. You're raring to go! Well, hold on now. Before you do anything else, you need to sit down and consider a few questions.

There is no one best answer to any of these questions. Your answers will vary from individual to individual and from group to group. Factors of personality, experience, church structure, vision, time, and resources will influence the way you answer them. But your answers will help lay the foundation for your group.

The first question to ask is simply, *Why?* Why do you want to start a group in the first place? It may seem basic, but your answer is important. Among the responses we've heard are:

- "I love to perform!"
- "It will increase attendance at our meetings."
- "It's a neat new way to preach!"
- "Well, the church down the block is doing it."
- "I don't know, it just sounds like fun!"

If your answer is similar to one of these, we suggest you (*a*) consider putting your energies into something other than a drama group, or (*b*) find someone else to take charge of the group for you.

Before you jump up to do *Hamlet,* sit down and consider a few questions.

But if you have a calling to serve others, if you are excited by new opportunities for communication, if you have a passion to see Christians reclaiming the arts, if you see talents that need to be put to service, . . . and if you are just a little bit crazy and don't mind hard work and long hours, then this "drama stuff" just might be for you!

Who Is Your Audience?

To help formulate the purpose of your group, you must determine who your audience is. Who will you be communicating to? Are they Christians? Are they members of your own congregation or from your surrounding community? Are they people who only enter a church at weddings or funerals? Are they of one ethnic or cultural group, or one particular age group, or are they a mixed audience?

Knowing your audience is extremely important. It determines the material you perform, the style of language you use, the issues you address, even the best location for your performances.

What Is Your Purpose?

Now examine your reason for beginning a drama group. You may want to answer this question yourself, or you might determine it after discussion with group members or with the leadership of your church.

However you answer it, write it down. This will be your *Mission Statement.* The more clearly and concisely you can state it, the better. Over a period of time you will find that a written statement of purpose will be one of your greatest assets. It will help keep the group focused, help others in your church communicate what your group is doing, and help prevent misunderstandings later on.

Not having a written statement of purpose is one of the biggest mistakes that a small drama group can make. Without a written statement divisions may crop up because individuals have differing visions for the group; while outside the group, people may have misgivings about what it is that you are doing.

Is the purpose of your group to be an outreach to the community? To aid in worship? To provide good family entertainment? To evangelize? To illustrate the sermon? To be an outlet for talent in your church? Or to explore the integration of the Christian faith and the dramatic arts?

However you answer the question, start with one focus. You can always add to it or change it as you develop. And remember, even if it is only one sentence, WRITE IT DOWN!!

What Are Your Resources?

Once you've determined your audience and formulated a mission statement, it's time to assess your resources. Do you have the necessary ingredients to accomplish your goals? Do you know where you can find that support? Jesus spoke of the importance of thinking ahead:

> Suppose one of you wants to build a tower. Will he not first sit down and estimate the cost to see if he has enough money to complete it? For if he lays the foundation and is not able to finish it, everyone who sees it will ridicule him, saying, "This fellow began to build and was not able to finish" (Luke 14:28–30).

Assess what you have now, or what you may have access to. Begin a list with four headings: *People, Facilities, Equipment,* and *Finances.* Don't let this overwhelm you. It is not a test! These are just some areas you want to think through. If you are only planning to do a readers theater performance every four months much of this will not apply to you.

People. Who can help you accomplish your vision? You will need to pool from a wide variety of expertise. Write down the names that come to mind in each of these areas: performers, writers, designers, administrators, technicians (carpenters, electricians, painters, graphic artists, seamstresses), financial people (donors, fund-raisers, bookkeepers), consultants, and various support volunteers (for phone calls, mailings, hospitality).

Build a team with a wide variety of expertise...

Facilities. You will need to know where you can perform, rehearse, build things, and store things.

Equipment. Lighting instruments, sound equipment, shop tools, office supplies including a typewriter or computer, and a copier.

Finances. What kind of a budget will you need? Will your church fund the group? Will you charge for any performances? Will you pay the actors? Will you reimburse any expenses?

Remember, one of the great features of drama is that you can do amazing things with very limited resources.

What About Structure?

This is a tough question to answer completely in one sitting. But, again, the clearer your understanding of the group's structure, the easier your communication will be. It is a question best answered with input from the group and/or your church leadership. As you think through the structure of your drama group, consider these areas:

Membership. How may someone become involved with your group? Must they be a member of your congregation? Will performers need to pass an audition, or do they need only energy and a willingness to work? Is there an application to fill out? Are there any age requirements?

Commitment. What kind of time commitment will members of your group need to make? Once every week for three hours? Five nights a week for seven weeks? Is membership ongoing or from production to production? Are there workshops, classes or Bible studies to attend along with rehearsals?

Leadership. How will the leadership of the group be structured? Will one person direct it all? Or will one person oversee the artistic area and someone else the administration? Will you have officers like many service clubs? Will decisions be made by group consensus? It's best for one person to have the last word in artistic matters. Theater is a beautiful collaborative art form, but it works best when someone has the final say.

Accountability. Your leadership structure will answer many of the questions concerning accountability, but there are some important things to consider. If you are operating in a church, are you accountable to the pastor, the church board, session, or congregation? Do you have regular meetings set up to communicate with them? Will they need to approve all scripts before production? Are the expectations you have for them, and they for you, clearly defined and understood?

Do you have your own board or advisory council? How often do they meet? Are the expectations understood?

If your group handles any finances, do you have a good accurate bookkeeping system? In what ways do you insure that the funds are used and the records are kept with integrity?

The Nonprofit Organization

Your drama group may work very well as part of the program of your church. However, there are some situations in which a group will want to set up its own nonprofit organization. You may want to consider this kind of organization if your group:

- will not be associated with a particular church
- will have a completely separate budget from your church
- would like to have an identity apart from the church

- wants to move toward a professional status with a salaried staff
- will be approaching foundations for financial grants

Simply put, a nonprofit organization is one set up to serve the public good and in which all funds are used for the operation of the organization. The staff is salaried, but no individual profits through stock dividends or other disbursements of the organization's revenue. Regulations for nonprofits are established by the IRS and individual state governments.

A nonprofit organization designated "501 (c) (3)" under the 1986 federal tax code is allowed to issue tax-deductible receipts to people who make financial contributions to it. If you donate money to a nonprofit 501 (c) (3) organization you may deduct the amount of your donations on your federal tax return (depending on the filing method you use).

You don't have to be a separate organization, however, for donors to receive a tax benefit. If you are part of the program of a church, people may contribute to the church and designate funds that are to be used for the drama program.

Incorporation

If your group chooses to set up a nonprofit organization it will need to incorporate. This entails setting up a board of trustees, writing out corporate by laws, and filing a set of articles of incorporation with the state attorney general. You will also want to file for tax-exempt status with the IRS. Get legal council from a lawyer that understands nonprofit organizations and your state's laws governing them. For more information on this subject look under the "Further Reading" section on page 259.

If you invest the time to think through, discuss, and answer these questions you will lay a solid foundation for the success of your drama group. Setting up a clear structure, dividing responsibilities, and nurturing the group can produce the benefits of a committed ensemble and an enthusiastic following.

Vaya con Dios!

"Unless the Lord build the house, they labor in vain that build it" (Psalm 127:1). For all your planning and hard work, unless God undergirds your group, all your efforts will be empty. You may succeed in outward appearance, but you will miss the rich fulfillment of being in his true service.

Keep in mind the Spanish expression,Vaya con Dios! — "Go with God!" Make our Lord central in your group. Petition his wisdom and blessing. Celebrate his love and his creation, and praise him with your best work!

3
Building the Group

Chapter 2 considered the *Why* of your drama group. In this chapter we take a closer look at the *Who* of your group. Chapter 4 deals with the *What*, and after that we'll get into the *How*. You will find the different parts of this chapter valuable or not depending on the size and focus of your group.

Ministry

Before we talk about the makeup of the group, we want to take a quick look at the word *ministry*. It is an often-used word in the Christian world—a powerful word. Yet, it is one of those words, like *bless*, that can carry so much emotional weight that it gets in its own way. It begins to have an aura of mystery around it, a fuzzy-edged specialness that can pull us away from its true meaning.

The word *ministry* is derived from the Greek verb *diakoneo* which means "to serve." It is where we get our word *deacon*. When the apostle Paul calls himself "a minister of the gospel," the literal translation of *minister* is "servant." A minister is a servant. And ministry is simply service. Try this: every time you would use the word *ministry* or *minister*, replace it with the word *service* or *servant*.

This simple exercise can help you see the true meaning of the word. For this reason we prefer to avoid using the cloudy term, *drama ministry.* Call your group whatever you would like, but at its core, think of it as service.

Building an Ensemble

One of the side benefits of developing a drama group is the little unexpected rewards. You were simply planning to bring a few people together to do some performances for your church, and now you look on in amazement at the ensemble this diverse group of people has become. The group is actually a model of the body of Christ—people with different gifts and temperaments working together toward a common goal. Talents are nurtured, discipline is learned, and people discover more about each other and mature in the process. The shy grow in confidence, the selfish learn to serve.

Theater is an art form based on collaboration and trust. A supportive environment where people have the freedom to explore, to make discoveries, and to make mistakes will be one of your group's best tools. Confident and caring leadership is required to create this kind of trust.

Theater is a team effort based on collaboration and trust.

Required, also, are individuals willing to devote themselves to the group and willing to focus on relationships rather than their own egos. This kind of team spirit inspires one of the theater's most beautiful creations—the ensemble. When there is ensemble in a drama group there is supportive, creative teamwork. Ensemble should be your goal, but it is not arrived at instantaneously. It takes time, commitment and a servant's heart.

Time. Someone once asked us how the actors in the Lamb's Players ensemble have stayed together for so long. Some of our performers have worked together for over thirteen years. That is a very rare occurrence in a business as ego-centered as the theater. Well, we thought about it. We are certainly not spiritual giants. We are often full of selfishness and sin. Our egos get bruised; we feel slighted or unappreciated; we struggle with envy, lust, anger, and pride. And yet there is a distinct difference, for as Christians working together, we have a mandate to reconcile with one another. We forgive and are forgiven. We are called to demonstrate to our co-workers the grace that God has shown to us.

All of this does not happen overnight. It grows as a group spends time together—time in rehearsal and performance, certainly—but also time in study and discussion of the arts. And time in prayer, reconciliation, and encouragement toward spiritual maturity.

Commitment. The commitment of time and energy by the individuals in your group is essential. Your group will not last long, or do quality work unless everyone understands and agrees to the degree of dedication required. If you have agreed to meet once each week for three hours, don't take that commitment lightly. Serve each other by being on time. You may wish to sign a commitment agreement if that helps to establish firm guidelines for all concerned. Use your time wisely. Set up a training, rehearsal, and production schedule for at least six months.

While commitment to the group is essential, be realistic. People have lives outside of your drama group! You want them to be uplifted and nurtured, not drained and disheartened. Remember, people get involved out of love. After all, the word *amateur* derives from the Latin *amator*, meaning lover, so an amateur is someone who does an activity simply for the love of it. But *amateur* need not mean second-rate. We have seen productions of the highest quality done by amateur groups. You may not have the experience, the resources, or the time that professionals have. But if you have the love, set high standards, plan well, and make the necessary commitment, you will be amazed at the quality of work you can do.

The "Servant" Artist

In our culture, ego is at the heart of much of the activity in the arts. Success is measured by one's level of fame and fortune. Celebrity status is the goal. The person with wealth and position is looked up to with an awe and envy akin to worship. Unfortunately much of this value system has found its way into the church. As Christians we need to present an alternative model.

At Lamb's Players, we approach acting as a form of service. The actor is called to be a servant to his Lord, to his fellow actors, to his audience, and to the script. He comes to rehearsals with mind and heart ready to explore. He comes prepared, yet willing to toss away his own ideas or opinions for the good of the play.

In an ensemble there is no type casting. The actors are willing to play a variety of roles, and the directors are willing to try an actor in almost any part. The actors support and encourage one another—there is no star system. This is harder to achieve than it first appears. It demands time and commitment.

Be a Team!

You can't do it all by yourself. That's one of the good lessons of life—and that microcosm of life, the theater. Whether your group is comprised of five people performing once a month or fifty-five performing twice a year—whether it is made up of volunteers who rehearse a couple of hours each week or staff members who meet every day—divide the responsibility. Your time will be spent more wisely, work will go more smoothly, and group members will feel more active ownership of the vision when the job is shared.

Though the situation and needs of each drama group are different, you will find some positions and responsibilities in the following lists that are appropriate for your group. Job responsibilities may be divided into two broad categories—organizational and production-oriented.

Organizational Responsibilities

However you decide to structure your group, make sure these general organizational areas are covered:

- Marketing or publicity
- Finances and accountability
- Communication (to the board or church leadership)
- Volunteers
- Records and history

Organizational Management. There are a number of different ways that you can divide organizational responsibilities. Some small groups have a general director that handles all the managerial tasks; others operate like a club, with president, secretary and treasurer. Larger groups often have an artistic director who oversees the artistic personnel and product, and a managing director or business manager who oversees administration, marketing, and finances.

If you have performances where tickets are issued, programs are handed out, or refreshments are served, you'll want to have a house manager. A house manager is responsible for the safety and comfort of your audience. This person's responsibilities may include lining up ushers, taking tickets, greeting the audience, arranging the refreshments, and cleaning up after everyone leaves.

If you plan to tour your productions, you will also want to assign a scheduling coordinator and a road manager. The scheduling coordinator handles booking calls, confirms performance dates, handles performance contracts and publicity materials, and sets up the touring itinerary.

The road manager oversees all the administrative tasks of the group out on tour. His duties include talking with sponsors, planning schedules, making travel arrangements, and dealing with meals and housing.

Production Responsibilities

There are a variety of tasks required in putting together a dramatic production. Each one may be handled by the same person for each production, or your personnel may switch from show to show. Here are some of the positions you may have on your production team:

The *Director* is the person ultimately responsible for the product. The director brings the artistic concept to the production and works with the actors and designers to achieve the finished work. (This position is covered in more detail in chapter 6.)

The Stage Manager is the theater's unsung hero. The scope of this person's responsibilities will differ somewhat from group to group and may include any of the following tasks:

- Running production meetings (described later)
- Locating space for rehearsal
- Reserving the performance site
- Preparing the room or stage for rehearsal
- Making sure the actors have scripts and rehearsal schedules
- Calling actors who are late to rehearsals
- Making announcements at rehearsals
- Maintaining the proper rehearsal atmosphere
- Taking notes on blocking, line changes, and light and sound cues in the production script
- Assisting the director
- Taking care of the logistical details
- Promoting clear communication between the director, the actors, the designers, and the technicians

The stage manager is the theater's unsung hero!

- Looking out for the actors' feelings, safety, and comfort
- Helping to find props and set pieces
- Organizing the "load-in" (set-up) and "strike" (take-down) of the set
- Making sure that any borrowed items are returned
- Informing the actors of the time remaining before the start of the performance
- Making emergency repairs to the set, costumes, or props
- Communicating with the house manager to see if the audience is settled so the performance can begin
- Calling the show—telling the technicians when to do the light and sound cues
- Running the sound and lights
- And sometimes (gulp) going on for an actor who has not shown up for the performance!!

The stage manger is one of a group's most valuable and important members. Treat yours with love and respect!

The Designers. Some of your productions will call for the use of costumes, sets, and lights. The *costume, set,* and *lighting designers* oversee the design and implementation of these elements. Chapters 8, 9, and 10 cover these areas in more detail.

The Properties (or Props) Master is responsible for building, borrowing, or buying the props that a production requires. If your production calls for very few props, these can be the responsibility of the set designer or the stage manager. If, however, a great variety of props need to be found, you may want to assign a person to this task specifically.

The Technicians. Some of your productions may have more technical requirements than others. You will benefit from the advice or help of someone experienced in the use of sound or lights. Technicians skilled in construction or electrical work can save you time and money, as well as assure you that these things are done correctly. With large set construction projects you will want a crew chief or construction supervisor who will work with the designer, assign tasks, make sure jobs are done safely and on time, and oversee the quality of work.

Other Directors. With some productions you will want the involvement of a *musical director* and/or a *choreographer.* These people will work directly with the director to make sure their work fits into his concept. The stage manager should make sure that any rehearsals a musical director or choreographer will lead are worked into the schedule.

Production Meetings

The key to a smooth production schedule is communication. You should hold regular production meetings. This is a time set aside (once a week works well) when all the people responsible for an area of the production sit down together. These meetings should be facilitated by the production's stage manager. At your production meetings you should:

- Make sure the director's concepts are understood
- Agree on the production schedule and deadlines
- Hear reports from each of the designers, the crew chief, the stage manager and the directors
- Foresee any gaps or problem areas and find solutions

You should start having production meetings, even if they are brief, before the production goes into rehearsals. It is often helpful to have your marketing manager, or the person in charge of publicity, sit in on these meetings.

Authority

It is important that, any timc you give someone an assignment, everyone in the group understands the authority that goes along with it. For example, make sure the people building the set understand that the crew chief has the authority to assign their tasks.

Take the time to write down a brief job description and the expectations you have for any production position. Make people's work challenging, but fun.

Be a wise leader. Keep looking for ways to improve the lines of communication within your group and with any technicians or volunteers who work with you.

4
Your Presentation

The important news flash is forgotten by the time yesterday's paper is in the trash can. The things we remember are emotions, impressions, images, and characters—the elements of theater.

—John Hersey

"All right," you say, "we have this drama group. We're excited. Now what? What is it we *do?* What do we perform?" The best piece of advice we can give you is this: *Start small.* Don't begin by trying to produce the book of Exodus! You will only discourage the members of your group, your audience, and yourself. The most common mistake made by a drama group just starting out is taking on a project too big for them to do with quality. So we'll say it again—start small! Do one thing well.

Depending on the focus of your group, you may begin with a choral dramatic reading of Scripture, a short story adapted for readers theater, or a short topical sketch. Doing one thing well will promote confidence within the drama group and leave your audience looking forward to your next effort. As you gain experience you may want to stay small or take on more ambitious projects. Either way, you will find more people excited to help you with their time and energy if you have put down a foundation of quality work.

Working in the Church

If you are working within a church, you need to work closely with your pastoral staff. You want to assure them that the drama group is there as part of the overall work of the church. Communicate clearly your group's purpose and goals, and look for ways to integrate drama into the life of the church. Drama finds its best use within the church in four areas: *Worship, Education, Outreach,* and *Enjoyment.*

You want the pastor and the congregation to see drama as a natural part of the church's celebration, education, or outreach—not as competition to the sermon or as a mere "extra." Discuss with the pastoral staff how the production will supplement the thematic thrust of the scheduled sermons or church calendar. These discussions will help you decide on the best dramatic form for your use.

Finding Material

Good plays for the church are rare. Good *plays* are rare! In the "Resources" section on page 243, you'll find a list of groups and companies that offer copies of their material. You may have to wade through a pond of the poor and the painful to find a script worth doing, but the search is often worth it. Send for catalogues and script information from some of the sources listed. Be sure to write Riding Lights in England for their great series of sketch books.

It may help to set up a reading committee. Hand out perusal scripts and anthologies of sketches to different people. Keep a reading list and cross off all material that is poor or will not work for your group. If a reader finds a good piece (or even one that *might* be good), pass that script on to the next level. You may want to attach a sheet of paper to scripts you are seriously considering. Here you can record cast size, production demands, and any short comments from each reader. With a large stack of "possibles" this process will help you find the scripts that the group will be excited about doing.

Before you go into rehearsal with any script make sure you understand the performance agreement. Do you need to receive permission for the performance? Are there royalties to pay? This information will be found at the front of the individual script or collection.

Some authors or organizations will allow you to make copies of the script, others require you to purchase one copy for each member of the cast. Some scripts may be performed without fee as long as there is no charge to the audience, while others require a signed license agreement and a royalty payment. Make sure you understand the requirements for any script you will be performing, and handle your agreements with integrity!

There are two other ways to get performance material: *commission someone* to write it, or *create your own.*

If you know someone who is skilled in playwriting or who has a good sense of dialogue, you may want to commission them to write some material for you. Clearly communicate any requirements you have involving theme, characters, or form.

Many groups find that their best work is the material they generate themselves. The great majority of all the scripts ever performed by Lamb's Players Touring Companies were developed "in house."

Other literature, such as, short stories, biographies, poetry, and essays can be adapted into dramatic form. Readers theater and story theater are ideal forms for adapted material. Material written in this century may be under copyright. If that's the case, you will need to obtain written permission from the publisher or the holder of the copyright to make the adaptation. When requesting such permission, state clearly the nature of the adaptation, your schedule of performances, and that you are an amateur group. Often amateurs are granted limited permission at no cost when no admission is charged and the author is given proper credit. Literature written before 1906 is usually in the public domain and in such cases may be used without permission.

Scripts can also be developed by *improvisation.* Draw up an outline for a story around a particular theme, and let group members improvise from this. Record the pieces of dialogue and story ideas that work. From this you will flesh out the complete script. Improvisation works best with short sketches.

Nurture the writers in your own group. It is a tremendous resource to have your own playwrights. They know the type of material you need, the deadlines you are working under, and the talent you have in the group. (See chapter 5 for a discussion of playwriting in more detail.)

Freedom of Form

One of the most exciting things about the dramatic arts is the wide variety of forms they may take. Just as amazing as the endless number of stories that may be told and the countless numbers of characters and themes that can be introduced, is the delightful variety of form in which these may be shown. In fact, one of the theater's great strengths is the freedom of its form.

Television dramas and movies are almost exclusively "realistic." If you find yourself watching a scene in a courtroom, that courtroom looks real. You don't see the false fronts and studio walls. You don't see the make-up crew and the bright lights hanging just off camera. The camera becomes your point of view, and it must show only what is "real."

Theater does not have this restriction. In the theater, a courtroom may be represented by an exact set, by flats painted like two-dimensional cartoon furniture, or by a simple table and folding chair.

Theater can be imaginative, abstract, or allegorical. It may be realistic or symbolic. It may present its audience with elaborate, detailed sets and costumes, or it may require its audience to provide those sets and costumes with their own imaginations. That is part of its power. Good theater demands the active participation of the audience's imagination.

Theater will also be either *representational* or *presentational.*

Representational Theater attempts to represent real life. As an audience we are unnoticed observers to the story. The set may be realistic or abstract, but the characters never acknowledge the audience's presence. We peek, as it were, through a window at the life represented.

Glenn Hansen and Sam Jenkins address an outdoor audience in the Lamb's Players Street Theatre production *The Hound of Everyman.*

Presentational Theater presents characters and ideas to the audience. Some, if not all, of the actors speak directly to the audience. There is no pretense of the unseen observer. There is no "fourth wall" between the stage and the audience.

Your performance may be either representational or presentational depending on the material, the choices the director makes, and the form you place it in. Either way, this choice needs to be consistent throughout the play or sketch.

One of the treats of being a small drama group is that you often get to perform a greater variety of theatrical forms than a large, established institution ever does. The big budget and fancy facility of a large theater can lead to a narrow focus and sameness, while your limited resources demand that you be more imaginative.

A Menu of Forms

Some of the many theatrical forms from which to choose:

Monologues—delivering the thoughts and emotions of biblical and historical figures of the past to our twentieth-century ears and eyes.

Choral Readings—helping us hear the truth presented in a fresh way, provoking reflection, and adding a new dimension to our worship.

Readers Theater—helping us experience the "color" of literature by adding the variety of sights and sounds that theater brings.

Story Theater—showing the reality of a spiritual principle, enlivening a parable, or recapturing the impact of Scripture.

Left, story theater: David Carminito in *A Parable for All Seasons.* Right, monologue: Robert Smyth as the leper priest Damien de Veuster in *Damien.*

Sketch: Pat Thayer, Don Lonsbrough, and Vanda Eggington in a scene from *Pardon Me, Christian but Your Old Nature Is Showing.*

Sketches—presenting a question to be addressed in the sermon or lesson, illustrating a topic for discussion, or helping us to learn while moving us to laughter.

Pageants—helping us remember our history, communicating our heritage, and celebrating our seasons and holy days.

Full-length Plays—exploring important issues, introducing us to remarkable people, and offering rich family entertainment to the community.

Street Theater—presenting the gospel in a fresh way, calling attention to important events, and confronting the values of an amoral society.

Some may work better than others for specific purposes. But get to know them all, and experiment with them as you are able.

Monologues

In monologues, a single actor presents a character (or characters) directly to the audience. The character(s) may be historical—an important person in the history of the church or a biblical character—or they may be fictional. What is important to convey is the character(s) have dreams and struggles we can understand and relate to; and that they can offer relevant spiritual insight into our present-day concerns.

Monologues usually center on one theme or event. Unless the material is very well written and the actor very accomplished, they should be kept short. Some ideas for monologues:

- Martha's preoccupation with activity
- Moses' insecurity about being the one to lead the Hebrews out of Egypt

- The rich young ruler's struggle with material wealth
- The Samaritan's choice to help the man beaten by robbers
- One of the men that walked by the man left to die
- Martin Luther's sudden understanding of Grace
- How Charles Wesley wrote "Oh, for a Thousand Tongues"
- A young girl caught in the abortion dilemma
- A man wondering what he has to give up to be a Christian

Choral Readings

A choral reading is the rehearsed reading of selections of Scripture or literature. The reading group may be either large or small. The readers do not usually move and the emphasis is on the meaning and emotion of the words.

For example, using a concordance, you could compile a variety of Scriptures on specific themes—prayer, repentance, creation, hope. Combine the sections of Scripture so that you have a beginning, a middle, and an end. Divide the reading into lines that will give the piece the most impact. Avoid dividing the piece verse by verse. Be creative. Make divisions by phrase or emphasis on specific words. Rehearse it to see how it sounds. You may find that female voices work best for a particular line, or that three voices sound better than one voice on a line you wanted to highlight.

Here is a sample of a compilation from the Psalms. Readers 1, 2, 3, and 4 may represent individuals or groups.

ALL: Sing!

1: Praises to God

ALL: Sing!

2: Praises to our king

3 & 4: Sing!

ALL: Sing praises

3: For the Lord God Almighty reigns

4: For he

2 & 4: Is king

ALL: Of all the earth!

2: From the lips of children and infants you have ordained praise

4: Your love, O Lord, reaches to the heavens

1 & 2: Sing to him a new song!

3: Your faithfulness to the skies

1 & 2: Shout for joy!

4: How priceless is your unfailing love

ALL: Clap your hands!

1: All you people

3 & 4: Sing joyfully to the Lord

2 & 4: Both high and low find refuge in the shadow of your wings

ALL: O Lord

3: Our Lord

2: How majestic is your name

ALL: In all the earth!

Because the material is easy to adapt and the readers have the security of a script in their hand, choral reading is often a good form for a group's first performance. However, even though you are reading from a script, you will want to rehearse for clarity, rhythm, emotional color, and group harmony.

Readers Theater

Readers theater is similar in form to choral reading but is more versatile. Again, the emphasis is on the literature being presented, but that literature can be almost anything, including poetry, drama, essays, short stories, or novels.

Readers theater is a flexible presentational form that works in a wide variety of situations. Although the material

Marilyn Mike, Karl Mertins, Robert Duckett and Vicki Smith demonstrate different perspectives in readers theater.

is memorized, the performers (usually two to eight) keep scripts (usually in three-ring binders) in their hands throughout. When a reader is speaking or reacting her focus is "up." At other times she "bows out" by dropping her head and focusing down into the script.

However, readers theater is not just reading. Performers may move around the stage, make gestures, or be placed on different levels. The script notebook may represent set pieces or props. It may be a tabletop one minute and, with a simple movement, represent a handbag the next.

Readers theater often uses the techniques of "offstage focus" or "cross focus." With this technique characters in dialogue do not look at each other onstage, but focus offstage across the audience, as if the character they were speaking to was at a point on the back wall. The readers' focus crosses in the midst of the audience making the audience feel more immediately involved in the dialogue.

This combination of descriptive language, (slight) physical movement, and offstage focus helps the audience to "visualize" the location, the costumes, and the look of the characters in their own imaginations. Because of the economy of the form, attention to the details can make the difference between a performance that is passable and one that is memorable.

For more information on readers theater, look for the books recommended in the "Further Reading" section on page 258.

Readers theater places the focus of the action in the audience.

In story theater, a narrator can progress the action. David Carminito, Dave Thayer, and Marilyn Mike in *A Parable for All Seasons.*

Story Theater

Story theater is a presentational form, which uses a narrative style to tell a story. The narrator may be separate from the rest of the ensemble or the ensemble itself may divide the task of narrating. The narration introduces characters, sets the location, and makes transitions in time. Actors may portray a number of different characters by simply changing their voice or a piece of costume. With story theater it is even possible to tell a "big" story with only a few actors and in a short amount of time.

One of Lamb's Players most popular touring productions is a story theater presentation of Dickens' *A Christmas Carol.* The entire story is told in fifty minutes using only four actors.

Pat Thayer and David Heath in a story theater adaptation of *A Christmas Carol.*

Bible stories, parables, short stories, and legends all make great story theater. Stories can be updated and given a fresh or humorous perspective. In our workshops with kids we usually improvise a story theater production of the "Prodigal Son." One group of eight- to ten-year-olds decided to update the parable. In their version, the prodigal son was twelve years old and instead of losing his inheritance on wine, women, and loose living, he spent it all on candy, transformers, and video games! Instead of getting a job feeding the pigs, this prodigal son got a job as a busboy at a local all-you-can-eat restaurant! It was great fun and it still made the parable's point about the loving Father.

Sketches

Sketches are short pieces (usually two to twenty minutes in length) that use a limited number of characters. While they usually focus on a single theme, sketches that follow a common line of thought or have similar themes can be performed together as a longer program. They can incorporate sound effects, pantomime, and choreography.

Good sketches are memorable. They can illustrate a spiritual or abstract concept, or clarify an idea. Good sketches leave a lasting impression. They move quickly and can end with a dramatic punch or leave the audience with a question that begs to be answered. In this way they make great discussion starters and introductions to sermons.

Comic sketches are disarming. They allow us to laugh at ourselves—to say, "That's me. I'm just like that. It's so foolish; I really do know better." Comedy helps us learn from our mistakes. Lamb's Players Touring Company does a short sketch as part of its program *Pardon Me Christian, but Your Old Nature Is Showing!* in which two women are passing judgment on an absent friend who is a smoker, all the while eating pastries like there was no tomorrow. As the two finally succumb to eating the cream puffs set aside for an evening circle meeting, the audience is laughing both at the fun of the sketch and in recognition of themselves. We get the point—how often we miss the beam in our own eye while pointing out the splinter in our brother's!

Note: Join the effort to stamp out the use of the dreaded word, *skit.* Skits are something done by crazed counselors at summer camp. *You* do sketches—and make them good!

Pageants

A pageant is a dramatic form of remembrance and celebration. Tied to a historic event, it may be the reenactment of that event or a dramatic reflection on its meaning.

Unfortunately for some of us, the word pageant brings up memories of bad productions with bathrobes and bed sheets. Because of those memories many drama groups have steered away from producing pageants at all. And that's a pity because a pageant that is done well can add a special dimension to the life of a congregation.

The Old Testament is full of pageants and feasts of remembrance. The Hebrews used these to recall, and to pass on to the next generation, the stories of God's redemptive action:

> The Lord your God has chosen you out of all the peoples on the face of the earth to be his people, his treasured possession. . . . It was because the Lord loved you and kept the oath he swore to your forefathers that he brought you out with a mighty hand and redeemed you from the land of slavery, from the power of Pharaoh king of Egypt. Know therefore that the Lord your God is God; he is the faithful God, keeping his covenant of love to a thousand generations of those who love him and keep his commands.
>
> (Deuteronomy 7:6–9)

The Old Testament is filled with the word remember in regard to the above events; and, today, pageants throughout the year can prompt our remembrance and celebration of God's good gifts. It may be the awesome judgment and redemption of Passover and Good Friday, the resurrection on Easter Sunday, the gift of the Spirit at Pentecost, or the Incarnation at Christmas. The important elements in a pageant are symbol and spectacle.

A symbol may be a cross draped with a purple robe, streamers of red cloth hung above the congregation representing the tongues of fire, or the Three Wise Men kneeling before the Christ child. Spectacle may be as simple as a procession of banners up the center aisle or as elaborate as a nativity story with live camels and angels in flight!

Pageants also give you the perfect opportunity to work with other artists. When well-coordinated, the efforts of

Symbol plays an important part in pageant. This is part of the opening pageantry for Amsterdam '86, orchestrated by Lamb's Players.

visual artists like painters, fabric artists, sculptors, designers, photographers, and filmmakers combined with musicians, poets, dancers, and dramatists can be stunning!

Full-length Plays

One-act and full-length plays provide a complete program and often give the opportunity to involve more people in the cast and the production crew. The greater script length, obviously, utilizes more of the playwright's talents. Biblical dramas, which are reenactments of a story or character study from the Bible, can fall in this category. Chancel dramas may be full-length pieces—usually written to be performed in a church or sanctuary. They may present the lives of significant Christians or address spiritual themes. Other full-length dramas, comedies, or musicals may be appropriate for special church events, family nights, or as an outreach to the community.

Francis Bates, Carolyn Schade, and Nate Peirson in the full-length musical *Tintypes* (Lamb's Players Theatre, 1984).

We are beginning to see the development of professional theater companies of Christians working together. These groups are producing a wide range of material exploring (from a Christian perspective) the issues facing our culture today. And many Christian playwrights are writing plays for an audience beyond the church walls.

Here in San Diego, Christian Community Theatre is the largest amateur theater organization in the county, and at least four local churches operate community theaters as part of their program.

Many others have dinner-theater nights for their own congregations, or they host presentations for the surrounding community. All of this is in addition to the professional repertory theater operated by Lamb's Players.

Street Theater

Street theater is a theater of the marketplace. Here you go out to your audience, you don't wait for them to come to you. It is presentational and confrontational. Its purpose is to introduce to its audience new information or alternative ideas. It is definitely *not* "preaching to the choir"! As a theatrical form it is one of the best for presenting the message of the gospel.

Do you ever find it ironic that in this country almost all evangelistic films are shown inside churches?!! Street theater takes its message *out* to people who would never enter a church. Done well, it understands the language, the idioms, and the values of the people in its audience—it should *not* shower them with church jargon.

Drawing Their Attention

Good street theater understands the theatrical elements called for in drawing a crowd. First, you need the right location—a natural gathering place removed from the competition from other activities and sounds, where people won't mind stopping to watch your performance for awhile. A college campus, a park, a beach, or a mall are all possible locations. If required, make sure you obtain any necessary permissions or permits.

Next you need splash—a sudden parade of banners, bright costumes, or energetic live music. You may even want to try an impressive display of juggling, magic, or gymnastics, or a fun, slapstick comedy routine. Be imaginative and present people with sound, color, and characters that are larger than life.

After you have attracted your initial crowd, you'll want to enlist their aid in gathering more people. One of the ways that Lamb's Players (we got our start as a street theater troupe) draws in larger audiences is, after a pre-show act, one of the performers proclaims:

Street Theater is fast-paced and colorful. Karl Schaffer and Michael Gregory in *The Hound of Everyman.*

> Thank you very much, ladies and gentlemen . . . and you, too, there in the back! We would like to ask your resistance in gathering a bit more of a crowd. Now nothing gathers a crowd so well as the sound of a group of people enjoying themselves. So, on the count of three, we want you to clap and cheer wildly and spontaneously—like you are having the greatest fun of your entire brief existence! Ready? One! Two! . . .

The sustained cheers and whistles often doubles the crowd!

Keeping Their Attention

Because street theater ventures into indifferent or even hostile environments, it must be especially entertaining, fast-paced, and confident. It must hold the audience's attention with split-second timing, rehearsed spontaneity, and bright energy.

Good street theater is both in control of the moment and flexible. This is where the confidence of the performers is so important.

Comedy makes particularly good street theater because it not only adds interest, but, actually helps advance your message. It has a disarming quality; and, because your audience doesn't feel threatened, they're more open to listening to and receiving a different point of view. Bear in mind that airplanes overhead, people wandering across your performance space, hecklers, or the sudden onslaught of a sprinkler system are all likely from time-to-time. Anticipate these things and rehearse likely responses for any situation.

One important tip: always heckle yourself if you are presenting a concept you know some of your audience will disagree with. Have one of your own performers attack the concept. By heckling yourself, you defuse any hostile verbal response from the audience and keep control of the moment.

Plant a Seed

A good street theater script does not give all the information. Its purpose is to plant a seed, to confront people with a new perspective, and to provoke a response. That response may be a curiosity to know more or the need to question what was presented.

Dialogue is an important part of street theater. After a performance on the streets of Amsterdam, Kerry Meads talks with an audience member.

One of your goals is to strike up personal conversations after the performance, for human conversation is the best way to communicate the gospel. That's why an evangelist like Billy Graham has hundreds of local church people trained in personal evangelism to serve as counselors with those that respond to the message at crusade meetings. If you do evangelistic street theater, make sure your performers know how to communicate the gospel in a personal way.

Street theater's energy holds its audience. David Carminito and Janine Zeller in *The Quest of Everyman.*

Be Brief

A street theater performance can be as short as a few minutes but never much longer than forty. Set up your argument and make your point. Don't be defensive or timid. With street theater you are on the offensive. While you are not out to blast and condemn people, you *are* there to promote the truth.

Learn the power of satire. Satire is a comic style that springs out of a sense of moral concern. It cares about its audience enough to expose and ridicule the folly in the culture that surrounds it. The prophets used satire. Isaiah derides the practice of idol worship. Elijah ridicules the priests of Baal. Satire has been a tool of great apologists like Augustine, Luther, and C. S. Lewis. In *The Great Divorce,* a bus load of passengers from hell pays a visit to heaven. Lewis uses a subtle satire in the meeting of these two perspectives to expose the folly in much of the muddled thinking of his day.

Our street theater production, *The Quest of Everyman,* is a fast-paced contemporary comedy set in the style of a medieval morality play. By holding up the emptiness of materialism, hedonism, and pseudo-religion, it offers a satirical look at some of the lifestyle choices facing us today, and then contends that true Christianity is a viable alternative.

Energy and color, costumes and sets help to hold a street theater audience

Street theater can also make good use of allegory. Characters can personify abstract concepts like pride or greed, hope or integrity. Bunyan does this very well with *Pilgrim's Progress*. In our production of *Quest,* we have diabolical characters with names like Bentbrain, Tallbrow, and Lust presenting drunkenness, pseudo-intellectuality, and sensuality. There are also the characters of Everyman and his buddy, Everybuddy!

Street theater productions should climax with a startling twist or a dramatic punch. Our production of *Hark! The Ark!* is a wild, comic look at Noah and the building of the Ark, yet it ends with a dramatic punch. After Noah and his family have gone into the boat, the building inspector, the sheriff, and a member of the animal protection league are left to ridicule him. Then come the first drops of rain. They run offstage heading for cover. While the audience is laughing, suddenly a large canvas sail rolls down and hits the stage like a clap of thunder. In the silence that follows, the audience reads the words printed on the unfurled sail:

> As it was in the days of Noah, so it will be at the coming of the Son of Man. For in the days before the flood, people were eating and drinking, marrying and giving in marriage . . . and they knew nothing about what would happen until the flood came and took them all away. That is how it will be at the coming of the Son of Man.

This always provokes prolonged conversation!

Good street theater is demanding. But handled with the proper preparation, imagination, and care it is a powerful means of communication and an exciting theatrical experience.

Other Expressions

There are other forms of expression in the performing arts that we do not deal with in this book. Dance, mime, and puppetry are some. If you have individuals in your group experienced in any of these areas, look for ways to incorporate their talent into some of your productions.

And there are probably theatrical forms that you can think of that we haven't mentioned. That's good—in fact, that's the idea! Think of more. The dramatic arts are as wide open as your imagination. Any form is valuable if it communicates effectively with your audience.

The church is doing a lot of talking these days. Talk on radio and television, talk on platforms, and talk on street corners. But remember something here—talking is not necessarily communicating. To be *heard* is to communicate. Learn the language of your audience; know their sensitivities

The church is rediscovering a wide variety of forms in the dramatic arts. June McGlamery, Nancy Parker, and Pamela Turner in Lamb's Players Dance Company.

and their values, their hopes and their heroes. Just as you wouldn't use church jargon to communicate to a college crowd on campus, so you don't want to alienate your congregation with material that is inappropriately brash. Don't coddle your audiences, but *do* treat them with love and respect.

Puppets communicate to all ages. Lamb's Players Puppets made a hit as Quimby Co.

Silence makes for powerful communication in mime. Cindy Hoback, Tim Wade, Bev Heath, and Danny Hartigan in Lamb's Players Mime Troupe.

5
To the Playwright

Why do writers write? Because it isn't there.
—Thomas Berger

We wish we had a dime for every request we've had for scripts. "I need something good to perform in my church," they say. "We wish we could be of more help," one of us always replies, "but there's really little of any quality available." "Well, what do I do?" they ask. "Well, why not write them yourself?" we suggest. A gasp. "What?!" "Why not write them yourself?" "I'm not a writer," they whisper. After several seconds of silence, "Well, . . . if there's nothing available, I guess *someone* in our church could . . . "

Well, that someone could very well be you!

This chapter is for those of you who have fallen, tripped, or been pushed into writing. "But why, me?" you ask. The answer: "Because there's a need and there's no one else to fill it!"

Anyway, haven't you secretly waited for the chance to exercise your writing talent? Now in this short chapter we can't give you a course in playwriting, but we can lay out a few principles. We can't guarantee that you'll become a budding new playwright, but we can give you a running start.

While the principles outlined here can be applied to

playwriting in general, the focus will be on writing shorter sketches—five to thirty minutes in length. A three-act play can be overwhelming for even the most experienced of writers. We suggest you start by writing shorter pieces; but remember, it is not the length of a script that determines its impact, but whether or not it communicates to its audience. Whether it be five minutes or three hours, the key word is *communication*—getting your audience to *hear* your message.

A word of caution here, though. A playwright does not write sermons. You may choose to write sermons, but that's a different form entirely. Most definitely, plays are *not* sermons! For when characters on the stage start sounding like they're preaching, the audience quickly starts yawning. *Not* because preachers are boring, but because the playwright is trying to make a play do what a preacher does best—preach. The focus of a lecture is the transmission of facts. The power of a play is emotional identification. A drama actively shows or illustrates, as opposed to passively telling.

The playwright is, first and foremost, a storyteller. She tells "the old, old story" in creative ways—keeping it fresh and alive. Her aim is to captivate, enlighten, challenge, entertain, question, and spark the imagination, all the while pointing her audience toward the Truth. She keeps the audience awake by presenting an important theme, interesting characters, and intriguing dramatic action.

Three Teachers

The three best teachers for any writer are *listening*, *looking*, and *doing*.

Listen. Hear the world around you. Hear the style of speech and the rhythm in conversation. Notice the color of descriptions and the accent of emotions.

Look. See good plays and the work of good drama companies. Read all you can. Learn from good writers.

Do. Write all you can. Do it for fun, and do it as a discipline. Write letters and short dialogues. You might try writing articles for local publications. Just write something, no matter how short, every day.

Keep a Journal

A journal can be an aspiring writer's best tool. It's the place to record all your mental notes, ideas, and observations. It should be a companion—kept within arm's reach. If you are diligent, it will become an invaluable sourcebook of ideas.

Put in your journal that unique character you saw at lunch, the fresh perspective on God's creation someone gave you, the fragments of an interesting conversation. Thoughts on things you see, read, and hear. Moments and people that touch your heart, grab your attention, and cause you to respond in a different way. Jot down character sketches and script ideas—even those great ideas that come to you in the middle of the night. (Remember to keep your journal by your bed so you can write them down immediately—you won't remember them in the morning!)

Spend a little time each day writing down your observations. Writing constantly is a difficult discipline at first. But make it a habit, and it will sharpen your perceptions of the world around you—its joy, its pain, its mystery, and even its sense of humor.

Beginning Tips

Okay, let's assume you have been offered your first project as a playwright. Here are a few tips:

- Start with a *short* sketch. A sketch should be long enough to illustrate its idea effectively, yet focused and to the point. Leave your audience wanting more, instead of being relieved that it's finally over.

- Keep it simple. Say one thing well. A simple sketch can illustrate a profound truth.

- Limit the number of characters. Don't burden yourself at the start by trying to write for a large cast. Remember, bigger is not always better.

Now ask yourself a few questions:

Who is your audience? Is it a Sunday-school class, or single adults? Is it a mixed congregation, or a mother and daughter banquet? Is it a church function, or a presentation in the community? The dynamics in each of these groups are very different. You'll want to use characters, situations, and dialogue that will communicate most effectively to your select audience.

What is the setting? Is it a Sunday morning worship service or a Saturday night youth meeting? Is the atmosphere formal or casual? Are there space restrictions? Will you be competing for attention? Will the performance be in a sanctuary, a gymnasium, or outside? Will it be in only one of these, or will you be performing in a variety of situations?

The answers to these questions will help you determine the best choice of style. For instance, although your Sunday morning service may be a casual outreach to members of the community, your Sunday evening service may be a quiet time of worship. Or, if you will be performing outside, you'll need to be bright, fast-paced, and loud!

What is your theme? Is the sketch to be a discussion starter on the topic of peer pressure? An illustration for a lecture on the struggles of single parenting? An introduction to a sermon on the fruits of the Spirit? Or a street theater piece on the emptiness of materialism? What is the central thought you want to leave with your audience?

Brainstorming

After you answer these questions, you are ready to have an open, spontaneous exploration of ideas—a "brainstorming session." You can do this by yourself, or, if you're feeling creatively dry, you can get a small group (two to five) together for it. One person's ideas can often spark another's and so on.

There are a few rules to remember as you brainstorm:

- No idea is wrong. Don't criticize or pass judgment on any idea. (In a group session, comments such as, *That's impossible,* or *That's really stupid,* stifle creativity and make people afraid to share their ideas.)

- Write down all ideas. Later you can come back to this list and choose the ideas you want to follow up on.

- Don't get bogged down. Don't go into much detail with your initial ideas.

- Make it fun! Be positive and imaginative.

- Don't go on too long.

Remember, you are not writing. You are only throwing out ideas—ideas that fit into the framework you have established by answering the questions above.

Restate your theme or central thought. Then use questions to spark ideas:

- What might happen?
- Who might the characters be?
- Where would the action take place—in a park, a restaurant?
- When does the action take place—twenty minutes ago, the next generation?
- What motivates each character?
- Where is there conflict?
- Should it be comic or serious?

When you have a good list of ideas, you are ready to sift them for the one you will script. Consider the possibilities—the how, what, and why of each idea. Will it communicate to your audience? Is it interesting or is it a cliche? Does it carry a clear central thought? Do you like it; does it excite you?

Through this process you can settle on the idea that holds the most promise for your group. This idea becomes the launching pad for your script. Now you are ready to make your characters speak.

Note: It is our suggestion that you don't try to write by committee. It rarely works well. Collaborate on initial ideas, collaborate as you move a script into performance—but unless you have two writers who work well together, only one person should write the script.

The Outline

Once you have your idea you're ready to create an outline for the script. Most dramatic literature, whether it's a seven-minute sketch or a five-act play, contains three major elements: *Theme* (or central thought), *Character*, and *Plot* (or story line).

You will almost always approach the writing of a script through one of these three elements. You may start out with an interesting pair of characters. Out of their personalities and conversation will develop plot and theme. Building a play around character is common in most modern drama.

Or, you may have an intriguing idea for a story line. The script is developed by laying out the plot then fleshing out the characters that it calls forth. This is the way most mysteries are written.

Finally, you may start with a clear theme or central thought. That theme can lead you to a story line that will illustrate it. And out of that, characters will evolve. Most sketches for the church will start from this point.

Theme

The theme is the central thought of your script. It is the concept, point of view, or principle you choose to illustrate. This will likely be the starting point for most of your scripts.

Let's say your pastor has a sermon on materialism coming up and would like it introduced by a sketch. From this materialism theme, you might write a script illustrating the foolishness of trying to "keep up with the Joneses." Or say that your youth director wants to do a Bible study on honesty. You could write a discussion-starter sketch about a high-school student caught in a lie.

The more specific your theme, the more focused your script will be. For example, take a theme of forgiveness. While that's a rather broad subject, we could narrow it down by being more specific. For instance:

- God's forgiveness of sin through Jesus Christ
- Forgiving a parent
- Jesus and the woman caught in adultery
- The parable of the servant forgiven his debt
- How many times we should forgive one another

By making your theme more focused, you will streamline your writing and strengthen the communication with your audience. (Remember, a script written with the theme as its starting point should be an *illustration* of that theme—not a sermon on it!)

The Character

No matter which of the three elements you start with, it is important that your characters are interesting and believable. Even if your characters are types meant to represent an abstract quality such as *hope* or *greed*, they need to be captivating and human . . . and not completely predictable! Look at John Bunyan's *Pilgrim's Progress*. All the characters in the story represent something else. Even their names help us see that clearly. Names like Pliable, Faithful, and Giant Despair. And yet they are all interesting people, not just flat concepts.

Your characters can fill a variety of roles in the script. What follows is a brief look at some of these roles. Obviously, not all of these will be used in a short sketch, but understanding them will strengthen your writing.

In *Pilgrim*, a fast-paced adaptation of Bunyan's *Pilgrim's Progress* by Tom Key, a series of antagonists try to dissuade the protagonist from the straight and narrow.

The Protagonist. This is normally the central character. She usually possesses qualities that are likable, attractive, or sympathetic. The play's action takes place around her as she pursues a goal in spite of opposition or difficulty. She is the major point of identification for the audience, the character they care about the most. Note that if you have more than one protagonist in a play it can tend to muddy the action and focus of the script.

The Antagonist. This character provides the opposition. She presents a strong conflicting force that threatens to keep the protagonist from achieving her goal. The actions of the antagonist create obstacles for the protagonist. The stronger the antagonist, the more the protagonist has to show the strength and depth of her commitment to her goal. The antagonist can complicate things in a way that creates tension and suspense. It keeps the audience guessing! Remember, though, the antagonist does not have to be a "bad guy." She simply has a goal which blocks the protagonist. It is not uncommon to have more than one antagonist, particularly if your protagonist is strong.

The Serviceable Characters. They mainly give information and make announcements: "Dinner is served," or "Mr. Graves just called and said he would be late." They tend to be service-oriented people such as butlers, milkmen, secretaries, and postal workers.

Left, the butler in *Charley's Aunt* is a humorous source of information that is crucial to the play. Tegeus, right, in Christopher Fry's *A Phoenix Too Frequent* is blessed with an odd, but trustworthy friend, Dodo.

The Role Characters. These are typical relationship characters such as mother, father, big sister, little brother, and next-door neighbor. Even though the relationships and roles may be generalized as "typical," the characters can still have unique personalities.

The Friend. This character shows concern for the plight of the protagonist and is often privy to her inner thoughts. She may clarify or question the protagonist's goal or motivation. She is often humorous or quirky and can be anything from extremely rational to highly emotional.

The Offbeat Characters. They tend to be delightfully larger than life; sometimes exotic, eccentric, slightly insane, and altogether outrageous. They bring comic relief but may also provide a startling but insightful perspective.

The Narrator. This performer is either a voice outside the story or a character who addresses the audience. She may give information about other characters or propel the action of the script quickly from event to event.

Yes, even bizarre characters can bring the truth to light. From the musical *Journey*, by Robert Smyth and James Ward.

Character Sketch

As you create your characters, remember that you are writing a script that will be *performed.* Actors will be interpreting and giving life to characters you create on paper. It is the playwright's responsibility to create characters that intrigue both actor and audience alike.

It is helpful to make a character sketch for each character. It will be a good resource when you start writing dialogue. A character sketch also helps you remain consistent. Some of the information it may include:

- name
- age
- social status
- personality traits
- relationship with others in the play
- attitudes toward others in the play

- feelings about herself
- strong emotions or opinions
- physical characteristics
- the character's "spine" (what she wants, what she believes in, what she will fight for)

Remember, contrast between characters creates interest and energy. It also helps to focus the individual qualities of the different characters.

Nature of Dialogue

While a script may use movement, sound, narration, monologue, or moments of silence, its greatest strength is dialogue. The verbal exchange between characters is what establishes the conflict and moves the action forward.

Your dialogue should be natural, yet distinctive. It needs to be grounded in reality—similar to everyday conversation. A common trap is making your characters talk in complete thoughts and sentences. This presents a stilted, unnatural rhythm to the audience. After all, you don't talk that way! It's perfectly natural to have our thoughts interrupted by someone else, by a phone call or by a suddenly remembered meeting. It is natural to have difficulty expressing ourselves, because we are nervous, tired, or simply don't know what we are trying to say. We often make discoveries or change our minds as we speak.

Look for creative ways to communicate information through your characters. Ways that they can give needed information naturally without sounding obvious. Remember, what will draw an audience into your play is not the information given, but the way in which your characters communicate that information.

Dialogue reveals character. Just as an actor's look and physical manner project her character, so does the manner in which she speaks. Each character has its own personality, and therefore its own distinctive style of speech. Obviously an Englishman speaks differently than an Irishman

Characters of the Wild West express themselves quite differently from those of the refined English countryside!

who speaks differently from a Scotsman. Each has an accent and rhythm to their speech that is unique. But there are many other factors that may affect your character's dialogue besides her nationality. Elements such as:

- age
- social status
- temperament (e.g., shy, aggressive, bubbly, cautious)
- education
- profession
- cultural background
- mental health

The situation your characters are in will also affect their style of speech. Are they comfortable in their surroundings? Are they tired or have they just woken up? Are they in a hurry? Are they emotional—hurt, angry, joyous? How do they feel about the characters they are talking to?

A character's role relationship to other characters will affect her style of speech. At a breakfast table a mother may speak to her six-year-old son, her fifteen-year-old daughter, her husband, her mother (by phone), her mother-in-law visiting for the weekend, or a neighbor who comes to the door to borrow a cup of sugar. She has a different relationship with each one of these people. She does not talk to her husband in the same way she talks to the six-year-old. The way she talks to her mother-in-law can indicate whether she feels secure around her or not. The way she greets her neighbor may tell us whether they are close friends or just acquaintances.

Each of these unique details feed your characters' personalities and that will help to make them memorable to your audience.

Action

Don't let your dialogue bog down the action of the play. It should keep your audience's mind moving, revealing more about a character, pursuing a goal, overcoming an obstacle.

Remember to show not tell. Presenting an event or confrontation onstage is usually stronger than talking about what has happened offstage.

Plot

The plot answers the question, *What happened?* It is the map of events, order, times, and locations. It is the characters in action. The plot is the story line, complete with a beginning, middle, and end. The plot may include:

- a specific chain of events
- a series of choices that confront a character
- strategic meetings between characters
- the time of the action
- the place of the action

A good script is like a well-prepared meal. Think of the parts of the play like the courses:

The beginning part of the script is like an appetizer. It introduces the audience to the characters, the conflict, and the style of the play. The beginning grabs their attention, pulls them out of themselves, and puts the world of the play in their focus. A good beginning:

- establishes the event or situation
- introduces the primary characters
- informs about relationships
- lets the audience know the style and mood of the play
- gives information about time and place
- foreshadows future events
- puts the action in motion

Every good script has a clear beginning, middle, and end.

Of course, you don't have to communicate every bit of this information in the first few minutes. New characters, a twist of events, an important revelation, can be introduced later. This helps hold interest and provides mystery or suspense.

What is important to communicate in the beginning is any information that will prevent confusion as the play progresses. An audience will lose interest if it is unable to follow what is going on.

The body of the script is your main course. This is the juicy part. It is where you develop the characters, enlarge the plot, or clarify the theme. It includes:

- growth or change in the characters
- exploration of the conflict
- development of new complications
- moments of surprise or discovery
- movement of the action to its climax

Your script may have numerous twists in the plot and various conflicts between characters, but it has only one climax. All the complications and minor conflicts lead to this final moment—the something that must be done, the decision that must be made.

Coming to the end—the time for dessert! It is the part of the script where the audience has a moment to wind down, put two–and–two together, or resolve the action of the play in their own minds. Some things to know about the conclusion:

- It may take a few minutes or be only one line.

- Some scripts resolve neatly, with all the loose ends tied up.

- Some end with a question mark. It's okay to leave an audience with a question, as long as you don't leave them confused. A question can promote discussion, self-examination, or be a challenge to action.

- A good ending is brief. It is not a sermonette.
- It avoids sudden, unjustified changes in character.
- It is a believable follow-up of the script's climax.

Note: Consistency of style is important throughout your script. The ending may differ with different styles. The ending to a realistic historical drama has constraints that are different than those of a short sketch on forgiveness.

Conflict

Conflict is the key to dramatic writing. It may be the conflict between two differing sets of values, a conflict between characters, or a conflict introduced by an event. It may be:

Theological—between God and man
Sociological—between man and man
Psychological—between man and self
Ecological—between man and his environment

Whatever its origin or its focus, conflict is at the core of drama. We've all been delighted to watch children at play create their own imaginative dramas. A doll misbehaves and won't do as it is told; army men oppose one another to be king of the hill; and the evil robots must be overcome by the good ones.

A friend of ours recently bought two toy action figures for her son. She wanted to encourage him to focus on the good and the positive, so she bought him two "good guys." Her son was thrilled at the gift. But he suddenly stopped, looked up at his mother and asked, "Did you get me any bad guys?" She said no, she thought these would be best. "Well mom," he replied, "what are these good guys supposed to do?" In his own way, he understood that there was no drama without conflict.

Opposition and struggle are part of our everyday lives. Daily we are confronted by things that would keep us from righteousness. It may be the temptation of material wealth or a lustful relationship. It might be the powerful voice of the world clashing with the values set before us by God. It may be the lie whispered by an inner voice that spirals our emotions into despair. It may be apathy to the cries of a neighbor, envy of a friend's talent, or a disagreement with a parent. The list is endless.

The Bible is an amazingly dramatic book. It is full of real lives and real conflicts. Paul speaks pointedly about conflict and its continuing quality in his letter to the Romans:

> I have the desire to do what is good, but I cannot carry it out. For what I do is not the good I want to do; no, the evil I do not want to do—this I keep on doing. . . . So I find this law at work: When I want to do good, evil is right there with me. For in my inner being I delight in God's law; but I see another law at work in the members of my body, waging war against the law of my mind and making me a prisoner of the law of sin at work within my members. What a wretched man I am! Who will rescue me from this body of death? Thanks be to God—through Jesus Christ our Lord! (Romans 7:18–19,21–25)

Our drama is most compelling and true when it contains the harmony of both minor and major cords. There is the reality of evil, the results of sin, and the emptiness of man without God. Against this backdrop is the hope of righteousness, the possibility of healing, and the powerful grace of God.

The playwright who is a Christian needs to *embrace* conflict rather than be frightened by it. It is in the conflict with evil that we most clearly see the good. It is when we see our hurt that we understand our need for healing.

Formats

Whether you are writing on a computer, a typewriter, or long hand with a pencil, there are several script formats from which you can choose. Here are two examples:

Format A

In this first format, each character's name is placed on the far left, followed by any stage directions in parentheses, and then the character's line. Character's speeches are single-spaced. A double-space is placed between the end of each character's line and the name of the next speaker:

> JEFFREY: (sitting next to the young lady, book in hand) The story goes that this particular inn was watched over, as the book says, "by a ministering spirit sent forth to minister unto them who shall be heirs of salvation." She was said to be . . .
>
> YOUNG LADY: She?
>
> JEFFREY: She, or so they say, was said to be a gracious and kind-hearted angel.
>
> YOUNG LADY: (crossing to the window) Is that what they say?
>
> JEFFREY: Yes.

YOUNG LADY: And who are they?

JEFFREY: Uh . . . (giving her a blank look) . . . no one in particular. It's just a romanticized tidbit of history.

YOUNG LADY: Meaning you don't believe in them?

JEFFREY: What?

YOUNG LADY: Angels.

JEFFREY: Of course not. (Pause) Well, at least not in this day and age.

Format B

In this format the name of each character is centered on the page and capitalized above each line. Characters' speeches are single-spaced with a double-space at the end. Stage directions are in parentheses and centered on a separate line:

JEFFREY

(sitting next to the young lady, book in hand)

The story goes that this particular inn was watched over, as the good book says, "by a ministering spirit sent forth to minister unto them who shall be heirs of salvation." She was said to be . . .

YOUNG LADY

She?

JEFFREY

She, or so they say, was said to be a gracious and kind-hearted angel.

YOUNG LADY

(crossing to the window)

Is that what they say?

JEFFREY

Yes.

YOUNG LADY

And who are they?

JEFFREY

Uh . . .

(giving her a blank look)

No one in particular. It's just a romanticized tidbit of history.

YOUNG LADY

Meaning you don't believe in them?

JEFFREY

What?

YOUNG LADY

Angels.

JEFFREY

Of course not. Well, at least not in this day and age.

As you can see, Format *A* takes less space than Format *B*—it can save paper and copying costs. Format *B*, however, is the manner in which scripts are submitted to theaters and publishing houses. Although you may not have any interest in publishing, there are still advantages for using Format *B*. It is easier for an actor to distinguish their lines from the stage directions. Also, there is more room to make last-minute line changes. This is particularly helpful when you are working on an original script that has never been produced.

Writer's Block

Don't be alarmed. Sometime or other it happens to every writer. You simply don't know what to write next. When this happens, don't stop! Keep on writing. Even though you may throw it all away, keep writing anything. Writing begets writing, just as brainstorming inspires more ideas. If you do get stuck, you might try to talk to a friend about it. Sometimes just talking through the problem and hearing another perspective will spark your imagination.

Have someone you respect read what you have so far. It is to your advantage to have an objective opinion on your script whether you're having problems or not. It's easy to feel so personal about your work that you are unable to see its shortcomings. Be prepared here. Your writing is very personal and criticism will sometimes hurt no matter how positive it may be. Keep an open mind and remember your goal is to do your best work.

You may want to assemble a group of actors to improvise on the scene where you are stuck. Give them their characters and the situation and let them play with it. They may come up with a new approach or idea that never crossed your mind. A decision, action, specific line, or an insight on character might open new directions to explore.

Throw in a new complication, character, unexpected event, or startling discovery to help break free. Complications can focus the conflict, give the action a sense of urgency, or revitalize a character's spirit.

Finally, go for a walk, pray, read a book, see a film—refresh your imagination! The short break will open new imaginative avenues to explore and release fresh energy for your work.

Humor

Don't be afraid to use comedy. Humor is not only entertaining, it is disarming. It doesn't threaten us. It allows us to laugh at ourselves and in that laughter gain new insight. It can break down defenses and present the opening for change. Even a serious point can be communicated powerfully with humor. It can be one of your most powerful tools.

Last Words

You want your writing to ring true. Write what you *know* to be true, not what you think people want to hear! This does not mean you need to write only from your own personal experience. Research, read, or interview people who have the expertise or experience in the area you're writing about. Write about what you care for. What touches your heart? What intrigues you?

The dynamics of writer's block is explored in *My Asparagus Is Growing Fine*, by Kerry Meads. The play is based on the life of Robert Louis Stevenson. "Some days we have worked from eight o'clock until four, and that is not counting the hours Louis writes and makes notes in the early morning by lamplight. He dictates with great earnestness, and when particularly interested, unconsciously plays the part of his characters." - Belle Osborne Strong, stepdaughter of R.L.S.

Writing itself is often painful, slow, and solitary. Make sure you have a solid base of encouragement and fellowship. If your church doesn't provide that, find (or start) a support group of other writers, artists, and people that have a concern for a Christian voice within the arts.

Above all, write! If it is what you are called to, do it! And keep on doing it. Celebrate your talents. Nurture them. Sharpen them. And give the results of your labors as gifts.

6
To the Director

I don't know the key to success, but the key to failure is trying to please everybody.

—Bill Cosby

Tag. You're it!

Now everyone is looking at you. You, the director. After all, you're the authority on this drama stuff, right? You're holding this all together. So now what?

First, take a deep breath . . . and relax! It is not as frightening as you think. First brush some of the expectations off your shoulders and remember this: A director is just a team leader in the collaborative art of the theater. Your job is to keep everyone pointed in the right direction.

In this chapter we take a look at the director's tasks, both in working with the acting ensemble and in the actual production. Although we discuss the mounting of a full-length production, many of the principles will apply to a directing assignment of any length.

Working With the Ensemble

Before we deal with the mechanics of directing a production let's take a quick look at some of the dynamics that go into working with the acting ensemble. Although you are responsible to oversee the entire production and will collaborate with different people, your primary work will be with the actors. A good director will do these things:

Provide Security. The most important part of the director's job in working with an ensemble is providing a sense of security. If the actors see that you have done your homework, that you know what you are doing, and that you have a plan, they relax. They begin to trust you. And a relaxed and trusting actor is a better actor.

As the director, you need to know the script better than anyone. Read it, study it, understand it. If you understand the themes, the objectives of the characters, and the rhythm in the story line, the actors can tackle their exploration of the material with confidence.

Have a plan for rehearsals. Chart out what you want to work on and when. Let your actors see that the time will be used wisely and every area of the script will receive the work it needs.

Build an encouraging environment. Lead your actors by nudging them toward growth rather than by criticizing their faults. Reassure them that no matter how much or how little acting experience they have had, this is a place where they can experiment and explore.

Even if you have never directed a production before, if you understand the material, have a clear plan of attack, and build an atmosphere of encouragement, your actors will trust and respect you.

Focus the Goal. One gift of a good director is the ability to look at the resources available and envision the possibilities. This capacity to peek into the future—to picture in one's imagination how a production will look—is a skill you want to cultivate. When you know where you are going it is much easier to direct others there as well.

With amateur actors you need to remind them that "acting" is not their goal! Just memorizing their lines is not the goal. The goal is to have the whole work communicate to the audience. To do that they need to understand and focus their character's objectives and stage relationships.

Make Decisions. A director needs to be open to new ideas and at the same time be decisive. Let's say a scene calls for an actor to carry a chair across the stage. Now there are two chairs next to each other that could be used. "Which chair would I carry?" ponders the actor. The set designer shrugs. "The one on the left," says the director. Why the one on the left? It's not important. You see, it doesn't matter which chair is carried. What matters is that someone needs to decide. A director makes decisions.

Although some decisions will be arbitrary, most will be based on a combination of study, experience, and artistic instinct. A good director has informed opinions.

In any production, the last word in artistic matters rests with the director. It is important to remember that he doesn't have the only word. The artistic input of actor and designer is essential and needs to be respected, but there are times when just one person needs to make a final decision. That someone is always the director.

Energize. A director is the head cheerleader! You have to believe that the work you are doing is important. Not always serious perhaps, but always important. Even if you are rehearsing a comic sketch with the primary purpose being entertainment, the work should never be frivolous or "ho hum." You need to be excited about the script. You need to be excited about the people you are working with.

If you are asked to direct a script which you don't believe in or a group of actors you are not excited about working with, don't do it. Politely decline. If you take on the project, your attitude will show through and discourage all involved.

If you are naturally a quiet or shy person, prepare yourself before you go into rehearsals. Give yourself a pep talk. Play the role of the cheerleader. Encourage; get excited when an actor makes a new discovery; be enthusiastic about a good design; praise improvement. Constantly remind yourself to be bright, warm, exuberant, and loving!

Energy is contagious. When you are excited about a project the actors will pick up that excitement. If you work with enthusiasm the actors will look forward to rehearsals. If you encourage them, they will be more inclined to encourage each other.

Train. A director with an amateur group often has the added responsibility of training. This chapter does not go into this area in great detail. If training will be a primary part of your work, you will want to read the next chapter on acting for some insights and locate some of the books mentioned under "Further Reading" on page 255.

The Four Cs

Whether you are training a young ensemble or simply directing one production, look for ways to help your actors develop the following four characteristics of *confidence, clarity, crispness,* and *consistency.* Master these and your group will take a big step in maintaining a high standard of quality in its productions.

Confidence. It is the combination of a belief in the production and a trust in the ensemble. Have it and your audience relaxes. It tells them, "we know what we are doing. There will be no need to be embarrassed for us!" It lets them know that you are in control of the moment. It is a quiet strength rather than a brash posturing or a hyper energy.

You can build confidence into your group through teamwork, encouragement, and adequate rehearsal.

Clarity. This simply means that your audience hears you. You are communicating. The character's objectives and relationships are understood. The actors' diction and projection is good.

Push your actors toward clarity. Point out sloppy speech patterns and muddy objectives. They want to speak with energy all the way through each sentence.

Crispness. This quality is achieved by paying attention to the details. The actors are committed to their characters and the story. Cues are picked up, physical movements are purposeful, and the pace is moving the story forward. Entrances and exits are done with energy. The rhythm of the piece has been established and set in rehearsal. The timing

of comic "bits" or physical actions is secure.

Consistency. This refers both to show-to-show predictability and to the internal agreement of performance styles. It promotes trust within the ensemble because the actors can count on each other to "be there" in the same way and with the same energy every time. The acting styles need to be the same within a production. Make sure that the audience is not confused by some actors performing in a realistic style while others are playing in a broad farcical manner. Consistency is achieved when actors have learned how to focus their energy and know the standards expected from each performance.

Be Yourself

In all your work with the acting ensemble be yourself. Don't try to be someone you are not. Don't use a directing method that you are not comfortable with. Every director has his own style. Strengthen the parts of you that will help build a good production and downplay the others. Remember to highlight:

- a sense of humor
- a spirit of discernment
- an ability to communicate clearly and to the point
- an aptitude for planning
- a capacity for encouragement
- an expansive imagination

Collaborate and Delegate

You can't do it all yourself! You are a team leader, a facilitator; you are there to help others do *their* best work. Your goal is to build the best production possible. To do that you need to learn the power of collaboration and delegation.

Collaboration. This is the combined effort of colleagues. It presumes trust and mutual respect. The dramatic arts are the most collaborative of art forms. The best productions are the results of cooperation between a community of artists. As a director you will be working in concert with a variety of creative people depending on the form and size of your production. In addition to the acting ensemble there may be costume, set, lighting, and sound designers; a voice or dialect coach; a music director or choreographer; and, on occasion, the playwright.

Your job is to present these artists with clear production concepts (explained later) and to keep the overall work on track. The amount of artistic freedom you allow designers or other directors will be dependent on their skills and experience. You may need to give more specific guidance to a novice, while allowing free rein to a talented veteran.

At times you will work with other artists that have more experience or training than you have. There is no reason to feel intimidated. Learn from their work. Ask for their creative input. But hold to your responsibility and authority as director.

Delegation. Teamwork presumes the division of labor. For the director, delegation is the assigning of responsibilities and production chores to others. It promotes ensemble and a sense of joint ownership and is one of the best ways to accomplish a large task.

Every production should have a stage manager. He should be your right arm! He can look after much of the logistic and administrative chores like drawing up prop lists, distributing rehearsal schedules, and setting up costume fittings. This way you can concentrate on the artistic product. He will also keep a prompt book. This book contains a copy of the script with any cuts or changes and a record in pencil of the stage blocking and any light and sound cues.

Set up a regular time before or after rehearsals to meet with your stage manager. He can be one of your biggest assets. Treat him with respect and praise his work in front of the cast.

If you don't have a separate production team, delegate production tasks to the actors according to their likes and aptitudes. If a script will need an extra amount of research, you might assign some of it to members of the cast. Or designate one person to be *dramaturge*. A dramaturge is responsible for research and any supplemental reading a script may demand. This may be especially helpful with a historical drama or a piece with a different cultural setting. (Additional production responsibilities are covered in chapter 3.)

Directing a Production

All right, let's look at some of the steps that go into directing an actual production. We are assuming that you believe in the script and that you are excited about the work ahead. If this is not the case, you need to either (*a*) go back and get excited, (*b*) find a script you can believe in, or (*c*) get another director!

Preparation

The director's motto is the same as the Boy Scouts'—"Be Prepared"! Before you walk into your first rehearsal or production meeting you need to do your homework.

The place to start is with the script of course. Read it and read it and read it again. Read it as many times as you can. It is your job to know the script inside and out.

First read it to understand the story. Then read it and jot down images, impressions, and ideas that come to mind. Then read it to study. You want to answer these questions:

- What is the predominant element in the script—theme, character, or plot?

- What happens?

- What is the central idea the author is trying to convey?

- Who are the characters? Why are they each there? What do they each want? How do they each feel about one another?

As you read the script visualize the action. Free your imagination. Bring the story to life. Make a movie of it in your head, adding a few more details each time you read it.

It is helpful to keep a *director's book.* Each director sets this up in a little bit different manner. Some keep only a small notebook to jot down ideas and research notes. Others make this an elaborate affair with one page of the script pasted inside a sheet of paper and a blank sheet for the facing page.

The director and the actors work together to discover the best ways to communicate the script.

This book will contain everything from concept ideas and character analysis to prop lists and blocking notes. Along with your imagination, your director's book will be the place to record your discoveries and map out your production plans.

Concepts

As you work with the script you will develop concepts for the production. The director's concepts serve as a compass for all the artists working on the project. They point everyone in the same direction. They set up the boundaries.

Production concepts are expressed in three areas we call *the form, the frame,* and *the flavor.*

The Form. In chapter 4 we outline a variety of theatrical forms. You will need to decide which of these is best suited for your production. In some cases the script may demand a specific form, in others it will be up to you to decide. You'll also need to make some additional decisions regarding the form. If it is a sketch or full-length play will it be realistic or abstract? Representational or presentational?

The Frame. The frame is the boundary established by time and location. All the design elements and acting choices need to be consistent within this frame. You would not have a diet-cola bottle on the set of a realistic production of the Civil War, and you would not have a wrist watch on Julius Caesar if the production is set in 45 B.C.!

The frame establishes which design elements and acting styles are acceptable and which are not. Think of the line from the little song on "Sesame Street," "One of these things doesn't belong here/ One of these things is not like the rest." The frame helps you spot elements that don't belong.

That is not to say that you can't have odd combinations in your production. They just need to be true to the frame. Our production of *The Taming of the Shrew* at Lamb's

Robert Smyth and Deborah Gilmour Smyth in *The Taming of the Shrew*. Directed by David McFadzean. (LPT 1984)

Players Theater had actors in blue jeans and Elizabethan doublets! There were sixteenth-century masks and hot dogs! It worked because of the frame. The setting was the deck and back yard of a modern home. Friends had gathered to perform Shakespeare's comedy for an engagement party. The odd mixture worked because they were true to the frame.

David Heath, Deborah Gilmour Smyth, and Rick Meads in *Saint Joan*, directed by Robert Smyth. (LPT 1988)

The Flavor of a production depends on the spices that you (the chef), decide to use. The flavor helps the designers limit their choices and find common threads. It can be suggested by a picture or an image, by sound, temperature, taste, texture, or color.

The flavor can often be best described by a metaphor—a single descriptive image. For our production of Shaw's *Saint Joan* we used this metaphor: Saint Joan is a spark of fire in a wood pile.

That metaphor gave the designers a starting point. The set became a modular series of various shaped wooden platforms built out of old planking. The costume designer outfit the cast (except for Joan), in muted browns, like a sepia tone photo. In contrast, Joan made her first entrance in bright red and was later dressed in green fatigues

Early in the process you'll want to hold a *concepts meeting* with the designers. Present your ideas on the three areas we have just discussed. Make sure the form, the frame, and the flavor are understood by all. After this meeting the designers will be ready to go to work.

Casting

It has been said that if you cast a production correctly, 80 percent of your work is done! But casting is not always an easy process. Every situation presents its own problems. There can be a great difference between casting in the professional theater and casting in an amateur group. The director of a professional production may have dozens of talented actors to choose from for each part, while you may have to cast whomever is available. Don't be discouraged by this. Remember, your people are involved because of love, not money. Your concern is for the growth of the individuals working with you as much as it is for the production.

Depending on how your group is set up, there are three ways you may go about casting. You can (1) *hold auditions,* (2) *assign roles,* or (3) *use everyone.*

Hold Auditions. You may hold open auditions for members of your congregation or for actors in your community. If you are working with experienced performers, you may ask them to bring a "head shot" (an eight-by-ten, black-and-white photo) and a résumé of their performing experience. You may also want them to come prepared with one or two monologues.

However, with most amateurs you will just want to have a *cold reading*. At a cold reading you have copies of a few pages of dialogue for the different parts you are casting. You will then have the actors read these aloud. Have enough copies available so that actors that are waiting may be able to review the script.

Most experienced directors will tell you that they can tell whether or not they are interested in using an actor after thirty seconds or less. Give yourself a little more time. Read actors for more than one part and in different combinations.

No matter what the situation, auditioning can be a terrifying experience for actors. They are putting themselves on the line. Look for ways to help them relax. Be warm and personable. Give them an idea of what you are looking for in each character. Have light refreshment available in the waiting room. Thank them for giving you their time and energy.

Hold a *callback* if necessary. Callback auditions allow you to see the best people together. Again, try different combinations. Give each actor some suggestions for a different reading to see how they take your direction.

Thank everyone for their time and let them know you will call them within twenty-four hours with a response. You or the stage manager should call every actor who came to the callback, whether you are going to cast them or not.

Assign Roles. You may have the same ensemble of actors working together from production to production. Since you will know their work, it is often possible to assign roles. Rotate types of parts that members of the ensemble play. While you will more than likely have some actors who excel in certain roles, be careful not to *typecast.* Thinking that a particular part can only be played by one type of actor, or that a specific actor can only play one type of a role, limits the work of your ensemble and over time will give a predictable sameness to your productions. Be imaginative; offer your actors roles that will stretch them in different ways.

Use Everyone. You may be in a situation where you will use everyone that has an interest. This is a great way to work with church pageants and large seasonal productions.

There's always a part for everyone.

It promotes a feeling of community and shared celebration. You may want to audition for the larger roles and assign others to supporting parts. There is always a way to make anyone a part of the production, even if it is as a part of the chorus or a banner carrier!

The Text

To prepare for rehearsals you want to divide the script into workable sections. As you grow familiar with the script you will find natural breaks in the action—a new character enters, a discovery is made, or there is a change in thought. These sections are called *beats*. You may break a script down into beats in any manner you choose. They may be as short as a couple of paragraphs or as long as ten pages. However you determine them, these beats will be bite-sized chunks of the script that will make your work in rehearsal easier.

From time to time you will want to trim some small parts of a script. This is common practice. Older dramas can often be too long, or too wordy for a modern audience. Many beginning playwrights have a tendency to write too much. Judicious cuts may tighten up the play or sketch nicely. If the playwright is working with your group, make sure you discuss any changes with him. Most are open to changes if you show them the reasons.

However, never change the intention of a script! If you feel the need to make a script say something different than what it already says, find another script—or write one yourself.

Most published scripts come with stage directions. These may be limited or elaborate. They are usually a part of the text, printed in italics or in parentheses. Look at them as tools, not as law! If you find them helpful use them, but don't let them limit your own creativity and imagination.

Blocking

Many beginning actors see their task as simply having their lines learned by the first performance. So too, many beginning directors see their job as simply telling the actors where to go! But as you have already seen there is much more to the job of directing than being a traffic cop.

At the same time, *blocking* the production is one of your primary responsibilities. Blocking is the plan of the physical movements of the actors onstage. Your goals in blocking are to:

- present pictures that help convey the story
- establish the relationships and emotions of the characters
- make the actors feel comfortable on stage
- make the characters' movement truthful

Don't wait for rehearsals to do this. You want to go into rehearsals with a plan outlining where, when, and why each character moves around the set.

For this you will need a diagram of the set. Some directors even work with a scale model to help them visualize the movement and the stage pictures they are creating. You want your movement to be natural, but not arbitrary. There is always some motivation for a move.

To determine directions to actors, you must consider what type of stage you will be working with. There are three basic types of stages that you may work on—*Proscenium, Thrust,* and *Arena.*

The different types of stages call for different blocking terminology. On a proscenium or a thrust stage, *upstage* is away from the audience and *downstage* is closer to them. *Stage right* refers to the right side of the stage as an actor looks out into the audience.

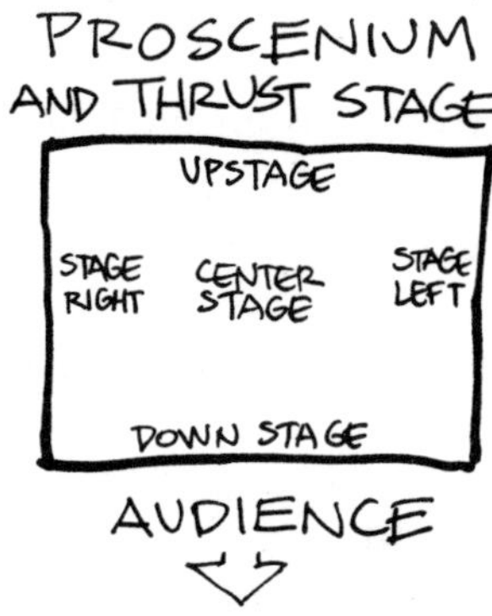

On an arena stage you will use *clock* terminology. Directions are referred to as the numbers on a clock. The center of the stage is the *center;* movement toward it is *in;* movement away from center is *out.*

Blocking is a collaboration between the director and the actor. Good blocking will always feel right to an actor, it gives him the opportunity to reinforce his character's emotion or objective. Bad blocking will seem awkward and make the actor feel uncomfortable.

As a director you want to be flexible and open to new

ideas, but you want to come prepared with a good blocking outline. You will complete the details and make any changes as you work with the actors in rehearsal.

Scheduling

You will want to sit down with your stage manager and draw up a rehearsal schedule. How much rehearsal do you need? Well, there *is* an ideal formula: One hour of rehearsal for each minute in performance. You chuckle! We know that this is not always possible but it is a good goal to aim for. Of course, different forms will have different requirements. Readers theater may need less, while fight choreography or pieces of comic timing may need more.

Decide which parts of the script you will work at each rehearsal and note which actors will be needed. Determine any schedule conflicts in advance. Take into account the availability of the actors and the rehearsal space. Leave some flexibility in your schedule, especially in later rehearsals, to work the areas you find need extra attention.

Include in the schedule any music or dance rehearsals, costume parade, or photo call. Also set a deadline for the actors to have all their lines memorized and be *off book.* This deadline varies from production to production but would generally be at the end of the first third of rehearsals. Have the stage manager send the schedule to the cast in advance or hand it out at the first reading.

Rehearsals

Now the fun begins—rehearsals. A common mistake of beginning directors is trying to do everything all at once. They want to see a "performance" right away so they give the actors the blocking, their objectives and attitudes, and try to polish up the timing all at once.

But a good director puts a production together one

layer at a time. First it has a basic form, then it gets slowly molded for more definition, then details are added, and finally it is polished and ready.

Early Rehearsals. Your goal in early rehearsals is exploration and discovery. That goes for both the actors and the director. Remind the actors that it is not a performance. While as the director you want to come prepared, you also want to remain flexible and open to new insights. Don't set your ideas in concrete, you are here to make discoveries together.

You will want to establish a few "rules" for rehearsals. These will help you get the most work done in the limited time available. Some expectations are that:

- everyone is on time and ready to begin at the time set. (If for some unavoidable reason you will be late, you will notify the stage manager.)

- there will be no "extra" talking in the rehearsal room. (Go outside to talk.)

- actors never direct other actors. If you have ideas talk to the director.

- no one outside the cast is allowed at the rehearsal without the director's approval.

- you will love your neighbor as yourself!

First Reading. The cast's first reading of the script together is always exciting. Have everyone sit at a table or in a circle. Make sure everyone has been introduced. You will want to take some time to explain your concepts to the actors just as you did earlier with the designers. Give some background to the script if this is necessary. After the reading take some time to talk about the cast's impressions and to address any questions.

Some directors like to have the cast read the script several times before they ever get up on their feet. Some only read it once and then jump right in.

Blocking Rehearsals

Blocking rehearsals can last a few hours or a few weeks. We have found it best to get them out of the way early. Many actors learn their lines as they learn their blocking and will keep their script in hand forever if you don't set basic blocking early. You might want to give a quick overview of where actors enter and exit and their general stage positions and then fill in the details a little more each time through.

Remember the movie of the script you made in your head? Use that to help you block the play. See the stage movement in your head and be willing to change it as you work it out in rehearsal. If you memorize the blocking you won't need to be constantly going back and forth to your director's book.

The stage manager should record the blocking in pencil in his prompt book. This will be the "official" record for any later reference.

Scene Work

Once the actors have their blocking and understand where they are moving on the stage you can start scene work. This is the time to work with the actors in each of the beats you divided the script into earlier. Scene work is the heart of early rehearsals. You want to make sure the following areas are clear:

Objectives. An objective is the thing or response that a character wants. Your most important task is to get an actor to make a clear choice of objectives for his character

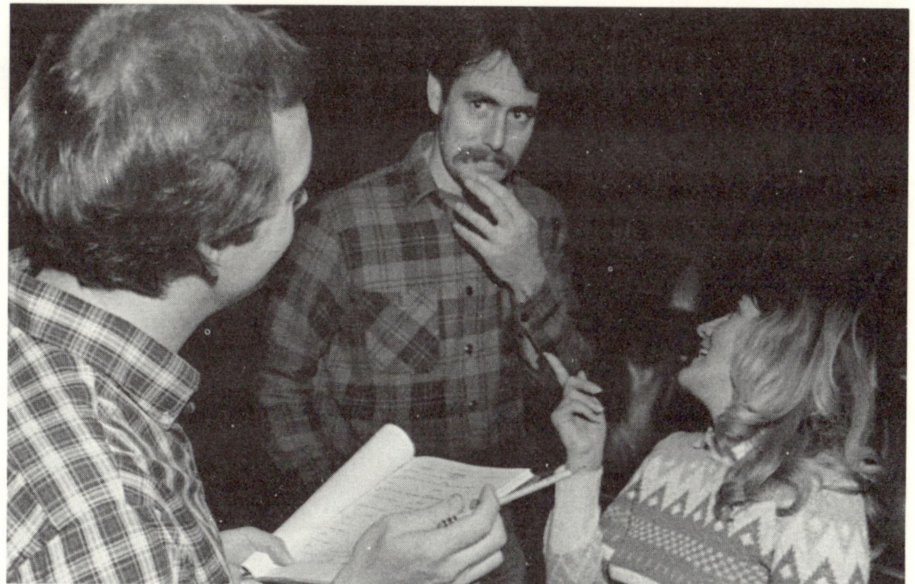

Robert Smyth at work with Lamb's Players ensemble members David Heath and Kerry Meads.

and then to commit fully to them.

- What does the character want?
- What is he going to do to get it?
- What is he trying to hide?

Actors can easily fall into "acting" a feeling instead of playing an objective. As a director it is your job to keep them focused on their objectives.

Changes. As characters either reach their objectives or are blocked from reaching them, they change. They may pursue a new objective, get a new idea, have a different mood, or reach a new level of maturity. In a well-written script most major characters will change in some way. Make sure the actor finds and understands those changes.

Discoveries. Throughout the play characters make discoveries—new information is revealed to them or they "put two-and-two together" and discover four. You want the audience to have this sense of discovery at the same time as the actor. Help your actor make their discoveries fresh each time.

Relationships. One character's objectives almost always involve another character. An actor is not alone. He needs to understand how his character relates to every other character on stage.

How does he feel about each one?
What does he want from each one?

A character is always trying to "give to" or "get from" other characters. He is always either initiating action or responding to action.

Giving Direction

Every director will have his own style of working in rehearsals. Whatever style you use, here are a few tips to build into it:

- Learn what each actor needs. Some need just a word or two and they understand what you are after; others need more dialogue and discussion. Some need a lot of encouragement; some want you to give them challenges. Treat each actor as an individual.

- Don't talk too much. You are in rehearsal to *do* not to theorize. Spend your time trying things, running things, exploring things. Don't get bogged down in words.

- Admit it when you don't know something. Don't pretend you have an answer to every question.

- Ask for ideas. Remember to collaborate. Encourage your actors to share their ideas with you.

- Stop the *I'm sorrys.* Many young actors fall into the habit of saying *I'm sorry* every time they fumble a line or are given a different idea. *I'm sorry* presumes that someone did something wrong. That is not the case in rehearsal. It is a time to experiment, to flub up, to fail. That is how you learn what works. So break this "sorry" habit. Besides it takes up time!

- Use action verbs when you direct. Words like convince, fight for, hurt, inspire, reassure, suppress, get even, encourage, destroy, win, help, figure out. These words give an "actable" image to the actors.

- Don't overload an actor. It is easy to give an actor so much information that he gets lost or frustrated. Work on one idea at a time. Give him time to assimilate new information or discoveries.

- Get stuck? Fall back on the motiving questions: "What are you trying to get him to do?" "What are you trying to make him give you?"

Run-throughs. As soon as you can, have a *run-through* of the entire script. Early run-throughs help the cast get a feeling for the entire piece and let you spot sections that will need the most attention.

In later rehearsals run-throughs are a helpful way to lock in the growth you have achieved in scene work. Run-throughs are an excellent way for the cast to build confidence and they allow you to see any areas that still need work.

Later Rehearsals

As you get into later rehearsals you should be making fewer and fewer interruptions. This is the time for actors to concentrate on character details and timing.

Play the moment. Push them to make fresh discoveries. Help them to "play the moment." Remember that the actor may know how the scene ends but that the character has no idea what will happen next!

Timing. The pace of the production should pick up as the actors learn the piece. Cues should come quicker. The only pauses should be those that have been purposefully set.

Entrances and exits. Make sure the actors enter and leave the stage with purpose and energy. Where has the character just come from? Where is he going when he leaves? What is he after?

Notes. These are verbal encouragements and corrections given to the entire cast. They will be your major tool as you get into late rehearsals. You can give notes at the end of the scene or the beat and have them run it again. In later rehearsal you will want to let the actors play through scenes without much interruption.

Be clear. Keep each note as short as possible. If the note will take more time to explain or the actor needs more dialogue, discuss it separately with him later. We suggest you give notes at the end of the run-through or dress rehearsal rather than waiting until the next day. This way they are fresh in your mind. It is also a good idea to have your actors keep a small notebook and write down their notes. This way they can review them again before the next rehearsal. In a run-through or dress rehearsal, notes will be your primary directing tool.

Encouragement. During final rehearsals a good director treats his cast with a balance of "pat on the back" and "push to do better." Remember to give encouragement. Don't just point out what needs to be fixed. Praise the actors for what they are doing right, and they will work all the harder to improve in weaker areas.

Discouragement. There is almost always a point where you think nothing is ever going to work right. You are certain that you are a rotten director, that you have a talentless cast and that you are working with a lousy script! Don't despair. You're not alone; this happens to every director. Persevere and try to see it from a detached perspective. At Lamb's Players the director of each production invites the other staff directors to sit in on a late run-through or early dress rehearsal. Afterward, we all meet to discuss areas that seem shaky or unclear and to offer suggestions which the play's director may use or not as he sees fit. You may not have other directors in your group, but you can ask two or three people who have gained your professional respect, to sit in just to give you a different perspective.

Paper Tech

If your production will have complicated light or sound cues you will want to have a *paper tech.* The director, stage manager, and lighting or sound designers are present at paper tech. You will talk through the entire show and determine the exact moment for any light and sound cues. Cues are written any time there is a change in the lights or recorded sound. These are marked in the stage manager's prompt book. (You will find more on this in chapter 10.)

Tech rehearsal

Tech rehearsal is where what the technicians have been working on and what the actors have been working on come together. It is where all the technical elements are added to the production.

Tech rehearsal or *tech* is for the benefit of the designers, the stage manager and any technicians that will be helping during performances. It is a time to make sure cues and levels are right—it is not an acting rehearsal! The actors need patience, for they will often be asked to run over problem sections again and again. Remind them they are there to serve the technicians. (Tech for a large scale production can last a very long time. Make everyone enjoy it more by having snacks available!)

Costume Parade

With a large production, you will find it helpful to have a *costume parade.* This is the opportunity for you to sit with the costumer and look at the actors in costume individually and as a group. Schedule your parade late enough in the production process so that the costumes are close to being finished, and yet early enough so that the costumer has time to make any last minute changes or adjustments you decide are needed. (More on this in chapter 8.)

A dress rehearsal gives actors the chance to get comfortable with props such as this break-away sign. Rick Meads in *Festival of Christmas*, directed by Kerry Meads (LPT 1987).

Dress Rehearsals

Dress rehearsals are run-throughs with full tech and costumes. This is where you will put the final polish on the production. It gives the actors the chance to get comfortable with their costumes and any technical elements. It gives the technicians a chance to work out any last minute bugs. With a short sketch you might have only one dress rehearsal while with a longer play you might have a week of them.

Don't stop the actors in a dress rehearsal unless it is absolutely necessary. You want to give them the time to find the rhythm of the entire piece. Dress rehearsals give a security to all the work you have put in. You might want to invite some guests to sit in during your final dress rehearsals to help prepare the actors for an audience.

Performance

Finally the big day (or night) arrives—the first performance! This is where you add your final cast member, the audience. Now everything is complete.

First performance or opening night is always a nice time to give each cast member a note of encouragement, flowers, or a small gift. You have all worked hard for this moment. Celebrate your teamwork and the gift you are giving to your audience.

A production can change quite a bit when an audience is introduced. If your show is going to run for a number of performances it's a good idea to give notes after the first few performances to make any last-minute adjustments.

After a production is up and running be careful not to badger the cast. You should turn the running of the show over to the stage manager. And you should only give a few notes if necessary. It is the stage manager's responsibility to keep the production *tight* and maintain what was established in rehearsal.

If your production is going to tour off and on over a period of time have the stage manager or road manager set up *pick-up rehearsals* as needed. These are run-throughs with the director (or stage manager) to refresh the actors' memories and to gather together any loose ends.

After learning the basics, the best way to grow as a director is by directing. Come up with directing projects for yourself. Assistant direct for someone with experience if you can. As a director you have the amazing opportunity to offer actors the excitement of ensemble and audiences the power and delight of dramatic communication. Take a deep breath and jump in!

7
To the Actor

Remember your lines and don't bump into the furniture.
—Spencer Tracy

This chapter will help you do that and a little more. It is written with the amateur actor in mind—the person just starting out or the individual who, for the pure love of it, has performed for years. In these pages we don't attempt to teach you how to act. Rather, we highlight some principles and techniques that we hope will give you confidence to explore further on your own.

Acting may not be as simple as Spencer Tracy would have you believe, but neither is it some vague secret mystery. Acting, at its best, is a disciplined craft. It is not so much putting on a character as it is stripping away pretense. It is not becoming someone else so much as selecting the parts of yourself that will best represent the character you are portraying. Don't feel you have to hide who you are—you are part of the rich fabric of God's creation. You don't have to *try* to be interesting, you *are* interesting. Work on mastering the technical tools that will help you communicate truthfully and be yourself.

In *Hamlet,* Shakespeare colorfully describes how to approach the craft of acting:

> Speak the speech, I pray you, trippingly on the tongue. But if you mouth it, as many of your players do, I had [just as well that] the town crier spoke my lines. Nor do not saw the air too much with your hand, thus, but use all gently, for in the very torrent, tempest, and whirlwind of your passion, you must acquire and beget a temperance that may give it smoothness. O it offends me to the soul to hear a robustious periwig-pated fellow tear a passion to tatters, to very rags. . . [Suit the action to the word, the word to the action. The purpose of playing was, and is] to hold the mirror up to nature, to show virtue her own feature, scorn her own image, and the very age and body of the time his form and pressure (III, ii).

A trap for many actors is relying solely on their feelings as their guide. Many amateurs think that all they have to do is go out on stage and emote! But beware. You may feel marvelous about your performance, having thrown heartfelt emotion all around the stage, yet, in actual fact, you may have left your audience cold. The wise actor understands that the craft is a combination of the heart and the mind.

The apostle Paul speaks of this balance in his letter to the Corinthians. Paul is writing to that church regarding the use of tongues in worship, but his words also offer insight to the actor:

> Even in the case of lifeless things that make sounds, such as the flute or harp, how will anyone know what tune is being played unless there is a distinction in the notes? Again, if the trumpet does not sound a clear call, who will get ready for battle? So it is with you. Unless you speak intelligible words with your tongue, how will anyone know what you are saying? . . . So what shall I do? I will pray with my spirit, but I will also pray with my mind; I will sing with my spirit, but I will also sing with my mind (1 Corinthians 14:7–9,15).

Acting is a discipline that requires the whole person—spirit, heart, body, and mind. It is a combination of intuition and study, of talent and technique.

Your Tools

A painter has his canvas and brushes, a sculptor his chisel and marble, and a musician his musical instrument. An actor has himself. You are your instrument. Your tools are your senses, your imagination, your spirit, your body, and your voice. Understanding the techniques of *observation, relaxation, vocal control, physical awareness, emotional identity,* and *imagination* can help you develop these tools.

Observation. Someone once remarked that talent involves "being aware of what others miss." An actor is aware of the creation around him. He is sensitive to sound, color, people, relationship, and conversation. They are all building blocks of his craft. The five senses—taste, touch, smell, and especially sight and sound—are important tools. Try these exercises in observation:

- Close your eyes and describe as thoroughly as possible the room you are now in. All right, how accurate were you? Did you leave anything out?

- Go into another room and study it for five minutes. Now leave that room and record all you remember. Describe colors, textures, sizes, placement of objects (in short, everything you can remember), in ten minutes. Return to the room to see how accurate you were.

- Study the physical characteristics of someone you know. (Don't let them know you are doing this if you can help it.) Note their posture, how they use their hands, the different ways they smile, how they eat. Now play a character using the physical traits you've observed.

- Go to a coffee shop and watch how people drink coffee. How do different people hold their cup? What is their pace? Choose one person and reenact the way they drank their coffee.

- Have a "color day." Place a dot on your watch or the back of your hand. Each time you notice it during the day, stop and note all the places where the color red appears around you. Change the color choice each time.

Observation is a great tool.

Relaxation. Professional actors will tell you that they do their best work when they are relaxed. When you are relaxed you have more control over your breath, your voice is free and open, and the dexterity of your tongue and lips is sharpened. To be relaxed is to be alert and free of tension, but it never means you are sloppy or lazy.

Along with overall physical tone, the warm-up routine is a key factor to relaxation. We advise that you make your warm-up consistent. You may want to develop your own, but you can also get help from a trainer, choreographer, or low-impact aerobics instructor. Begin your routine slowly and gently, being careful to avoid over-stretching or pulling muscles. Here are some of our suggestions:

1. Stretch and open your face, mouth, and eyes as wide as possible. Then do the opposite—pull your face, mouth, and eyes in, pursing them together to make your face as small as possible.

2. Slowly drop your head to your chest (feel the stretch in the back of your neck), then roll your head slowly in a circular motion. Now reverse the direction. Finally, drop your head slowly from side–to–side, ear–to–shoulder.

3. Roll your shoulders forward, then backward, in a circular motion. Pull shoulders up and then release down.

4. Swing your arms in slow circles, first forward, then back.

5. Push-ups are great for waking up and toning the arms. Keep your neck relaxed, looking at the floor in front of you, your hips in line so you don't put pressure on your lower back.

6. Stand with feet at shoulder width and stretch

your right arm up, your hand reaching for the ceiling above your left shoulder. Alternate from side to side.

7. Standing straight, let your head drop forward. Now continue bending forward toward the floor. Your knees are bent and your arms are hanging loosely like a rag doll's. As you bend forward, try to feel each vertebra release. Reverse and slowly rise to a standing position.

8. Do moderate sit-ups with knees bent to avoid putting strain on your back.

9. Sit on the floor "Indian style" and stretch your arms forward, feeling the stretch in your lower back. With your legs in the same position, turn your torso slowly to the left and to the right, feeling the stretch in your lower back.

10. On the floor, legs straight in front of you, stretch forward and reach for your toes. Repeat this with toes pointed forward (feel the stretch in the back of your legs) and toes flexed (feel the stretch in the back of your calves).

11. On the floor, open the legs (only as far as you are comfortable) and reach from side-to-side, trying to touch your toes. Then reach straight ahead.

12. Walk in place, shifting your weight from one foot to the other. Stretch the ankles and the muscles in the foot by slowly raising and lowering your heels while the feet stay in place.

Vocal Control. Remember Shakespeare's memorable thoughts on communication in *Hamlet,* that we quoted before: "Speak the speech, I pray you, as I pronounced it to you, trippingly on the tongue." We Americans often tend to be sloppy or casual in our speech, and often carry these habits into performance.

Cecily Berry, voice coach for the Royal Shakespeare Company, wrote a wonderful book, *Voice and the Actor.* It is a valuable resource to have handy. However, overcoming speech or vocal problems can sometimes be difficult without a voice coach or an objective ear. You can find personal instruction at a local college or with a private voice coach.

Breath control, resonance, projection, diction, and *accent* are all important elements in the communication of a thought or a feeling.

Breath Control. Breath is the fuel for the voice. Without breath we cannot make a sound! The more breath support you have the more solid the sound. Place your hands on the lower front of your rib cage. Take a deep breath. You should feel your lower ribs expand with each breath. Now place your hands on the back of your rib cage. Take a deep breath. Again, you should feel your back expand with each breath. These ribs move to make room for the lungs as they fill to capacity. If you find that your chest is moving up and down, rather than your lower ribs moving in and out, you are not breathing as deeply as you are able. Breathe until your stomach expands. This puts your diaphragm to best use, and will give you more breath support.

Exercises:

1. Lie on your back on the floor with your knees bent and pointed toward the ceiling. Relax the small of your back allowing it to spread and touch the floor. Don't push or strain.

2. One at a time relax the shoulders, the back of the neck, the arms, the hands, and the fingers. Imagine that you are lying in something soothing like cool grass or tropical water.

3. Let your head roll easily from side-to-side. Don't force it—concentrate on freeing the tension.

4. Place your hands on the lower rib cage and take in a long, relaxed breath through your nose. Feel the expansion in your abdomen. Breathe out with an open mouth. Repeat this several times, releasing tension each time you exhale.

5. Many people carry a great deal of tension in their neck, jaws, and shoulders. This tension has an affect on the throat and voice. Let your jaw drop open naturally—don't force any movement. Try to touch your nose, cheeks, and chin with your tongue.

6. Breathe in through your nose. Exhale through your mouth with a humming sound. Turn the hum to an *ah* sound halfway through your exhale—(*"mmmmm....ahhhh"*).

7. Repeat, this time placing your tongue just behind (but not touching) your upper teeth. Make an *ll* sound opening to the *ah* sound with each exhalation—(*"llll...aahhh"*).

8. Repeat this going through all the consonants.

Resonance. When you speak, the bones and tissues in your head and chest act as resonators. Hum for a minute. You can feel the vibrations in your mouth, nose, facial muscles, and ribs. Resonance is what gives your voice much of its pitch, color, and texture. Experiment with this. Try placing your voice at different points of resonance. The control of vocal pitch will give you more variety as an actor.

Projection is the clear communication of your lines to your entire audience. It is not just volume, but the controlled display of vocal power. It is achieved with good breath support, firm resonance, and an open vocal passage.

Diction. Vowel and consonant sounds combine to create the words we use to communicate. It is important for an actor to make his communication clear. Regional dialects often affect the clarity of our speech. We may speak with a dialect unique to our immediate part of the country: rounded vowels are common in the upper Midwest, a graceful drawl is a familiar sound in the South. You may not hear the dialect in your own speech, but tape your normal voice and you may be surprised at the patterns in your own speech. Listen to the subtle nuance of speech in your friends and family. You can develop your ear by detecting unusual speech patterns in others.

The best way to become sensitized to diction is to play with the sounds that make up language. Consonants are either *plosive* or *continuant.* Plosive consonants are just like they sound—explosive, as in *b, d, f, g,* and *k.* Continuant consonants beg to be continued, as in *l, m, n, r* and *s.*

Exercises:

1. Speak the following clearly:

Bee, bay, bah, boh, boo
Dee, day, dah, doh, doo
Fee, fay, fah, foh, foo

2. Go through all the consonants like this. Try to sing it.

3. Tongue Twisters are ideal for diction and vocal warm-ups. Here are some of our favorites. Repeat them several times quickly and distinctly. Concentrate on ones that are the hardest for you.

- Babbling baby Bobby bobbles the bimble bobbles on his bib.
- Kiki, the cuckoo, cuts capers, clowning cleverly, and calling to the kitchen clock.
- Don didn't do the difficult, dangerous deeds that Dickie did.
- Few folks find the fine flavor from fried fritters that Freda finds.
- Good guys grunt, glare, grab, or growl, in governments governed by gloomy goons.
- Happy Harry Harding, harassed by hippy Haley Hatter, hit hippy Haley's hairy head.
- Jim, Jill, Jane, and Johnny jammed jollily in a juiced Jaguar, just jetted Jack's Jeep like jumping Jupiter.

- Languid little Lillian, living by the lily pond, lets little lazy lizards lie along the lily pads.
- Many money-minded moguls mind their moola more than morals.
- Nine nice nieces, neatly nibbling on knick-knacks, never noticed nine nice nephews, noticing nine nice nieces.
- Popular people, peopling popular places, place popular places in precarious positions, by populating places with a plethora of people.
- The Right Reverend Randolph Ransome Right is rarely wrong, rather right, when really writing religious rites.
- Sheila shall surely show her shining seashore shells, shan't she?
- Tiny Teddy Tucker troubles not to toot his tooter, 'til Teddy's tutor told Teddy Tucker the time to toot his tooter was today!
- Wanda Winkle whispered *whether, wither, whence* while wondering when, and where, and which.
- To sit in solemn silence in a dull, dark dock, in a pestilential prison with a lifelong lock, awaiting the sensation of a short, sharp shock, from a cheap and chippy chopper on a big, black block!

Accent. Many characters require a regional dialect or accent. Even when a script does not specifically call for it, a slight accent may add an interesting spice to your character now and then. The best way to learn a dialect or accent is to listen. Listen to the music in the voices around you, then listen some more! Copy the sound. Hear the variation in the vowel and consonant sounds. We also recommend *Stage Dialects*, a book and tape series by Jerry Blunt (see "Further Reading," on page 255). It is a very effective system. Remember that your primary focus is clear communication, not a completely accurate accent. A small, consistent flavor or rhythm of an accent will often convey the complete accent and still keep your speech understandable.

Take care with accents, however. There is nothing more distracting to a character than a bad or inconsistent accent. It is better to use no accent, even if it is called for by the script, then to use one poorly.

Practice by reading aloud whenever you can. Practice diction; vary your pitch; experiment with emotion. Reading aloud can put put you in touch with language like nothing else can. Good selections can be found in Shakespeare, Milton, Poe, Donne, or the Psalms.

Gerard Manley Hopkins' poem, "The Windhover," illustrates a delicious love for the sound of words and the way it can strengthen communication:

THE WINDHOVER: To Christ our Lord

I caught this morning morning's minion, kingdom of day-
light's dauphin, dapple-dawn-drawn Falcon, in his
riding
Of the rolling level underneath him steady air, and striding
High there, how he rung upon the rein of a wimpling wing
In his ecstasy! then off, off forth on swing,
As a skate's heel sweeps smooth on a bow-bend: the hurl
and gliding
Rebuffed the big wind. My heart in hiding
Stirred for a bird—the achieve of, the mastery of the thing!

Brute beauty and valour and act, oh, air, pride, plume, here
Buckle! and the fire that breaks from thee then, a billion
Times told lovelier, more dangerous, O my chevalier!
No wonder of it: sheer plod makes plough down sillion
Shine, and blue-bleak embers, ah my dear,
Fall, gall themselves, and gash gold-vermilion.

Emotional Identity. You want your character to have emotional validity. Now, this does not mean that you, the actor, need to feel exactly what the character feels! But it is important that you understand, relate to, and empathize with the character's feelings. Your job is to create a believable character for the audience.

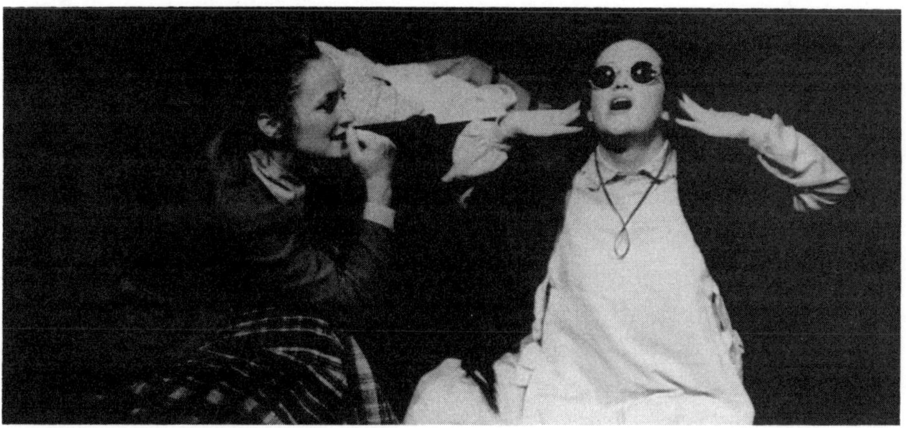

In *The Miracle Worker*, the actor must learn to empathize with the feelings and needs of a blind person.

Analyze your character's basic emotional needs. Do they seek acceptance, enjoyment, control, peace? Their emotional needs are often colored by their motivations. Ask yourself what motivates your character. Why does he or she respond that particular way? Are they trying to hide something? Are they protecting something? Are they trying to get something?

How do they express their emotions? Do they show them quickly? Do they fight to hide them? Are they dramatic? Do they hold a grudge? Does the emotion flare and then pass quickly?

Are they comfortable with their emotions, or not? The impact of an outburst of joy or anger from a character who is normally subdued and "unemotional" is quite different from the display of emotion that comes from one who is always irritated with life. It is important that you understand both the emotional temperament of the character and the emotion of the given moment in the scene you are playing. The surrounding situation is also important. A piece of bread to a starving man has much more significance than a grand meal to a king. So it is with emotion. Keep the response in proportion to the character's needs and the scene in which it is played.

Using your own emotional memories can help you find a bridge—an understanding of your character's feelings. How can you relate to what he feels and the way he responds? Emotions are complex and odd things can trigger them including sights, sounds, and smells. The more you are in touch with your own emotions the more they can become tools to communicate your character's emotions to your audience.

For example, your character may have just experienced the death of a parent. Perhaps you never have, but by recalling a time when you did experience a strong emotion of loss you have a glimpse into your character's feelings.

Or your character may have just learned that he has been accepted at a military academy—a place he has long desired to go. Perhaps you cannot relate to the measure of his exuberance on receiving the acceptance. Find a moment in your own experience that will help duplicate the picture of excitement that your character feels. This could be as simple as the flush you experience on your first day of a long-awaited vacation.

Understanding the emotional make up of a character helps you select vocal and physical actions that are truthful for that character. Try this group exercise: Have the group sit in a circle. One person will start to pass an imaginary "photo" around the circle. Each person takes the photo,

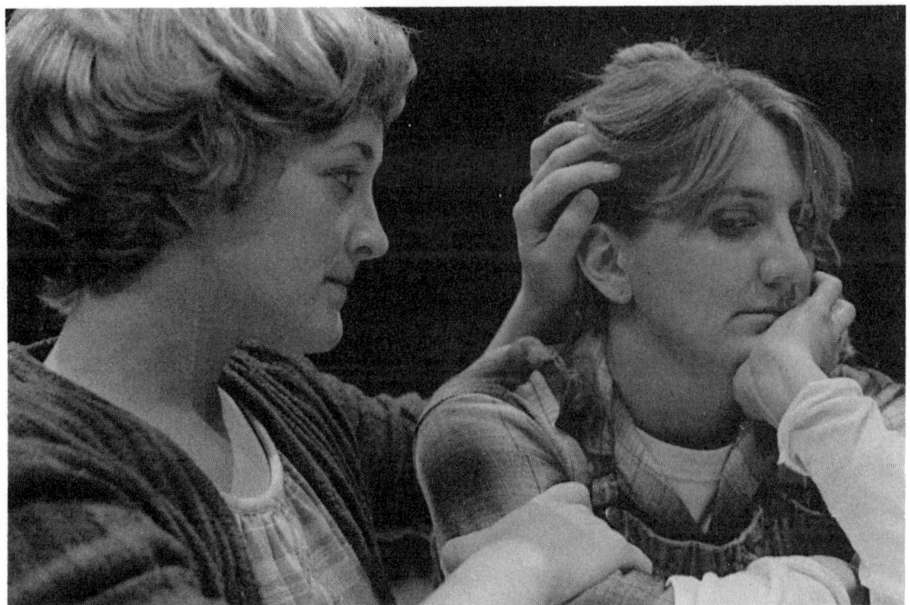

The emotional tensions between mother and daughter are subtly explored in *Deep River* by David McFadzean.

"sees" it, and passes it on. First, it is a picture of your best friend; then a photo of your mother, a pet from long ago, a stranger; and, finally, someone who hurt you. Don't "act" your response—the object is to discover the emotion you feel with each photo you see.

Use discretion in the display of emotion on stage. Pushing too far, or putting on a grand emotion can make your character unbelievable. Sometimes hiding the emotion—underplaying it—is a stronger choice than letting it loose.

Note: Look at the display of anger on stage as a spice. Don't overdo it. It will not sustain interest for long. Use it with care.

Physical Awareness. A common mistake of amateurs is thinking that all there is to acting is saying lines. But if you don't want to "bump into the furniture," you need to be aware of how your physical presence plays a part in acting.

The physical choices you make communicate a lot about the personality and emotional state of the character. Rapid, nervous pacing communicates something strikingly different from a slow deliberate turn of the head.

When building characters for the stage, take the time to think through, rehearse, and settle on their physical traits. This can be wonderfully fun. How would they walk? What is there posture like? Would they have any nervous or unusual physical habits? If your character eats onstage how would they hold their fork or cup? Would they slurp their coffee? Are they shy or extroverted, self-conscious, or abandoned?

Observation can be a good source for ideas:

- A zoo is a great place; there is a wealth of possibility here. By modifying an animal's movement, you can find new ways to walk, move your head, or stand.

- Watch children in a playground and you will learn some wonderfully free and imaginative movement.

- Try machine-like movement for unusual variations of movement.

Exercises:

1. Memorize a monologue and practice it, giving your character the physical traits of a tiger, then an elephant, and, finally, a mouse.

2. Find a large portrait of a character that interests you. Place it next to a mirror. Notice the ways in which their facial structure is different from yours. Now, by using the muscles in your face, try to make your appearance more like theirs.

Your goal in building a physical character is to make it your own. You don't have to make choices that are "normal," but you do have to "own" the choices that you settle on—you have to be committed to a consistent representation of the character.

Importance of Text

It is in the script of the play or sketch that the actor discovers the life of their character. From the moment the actor receives the script until the first performance, much time should be spent reading and re-reading it for the meat it holds.

The story becomes the framework to understanding your character. When you read the script, pay attention to *what* happens and *why* it happens. If it helps you, draft a simple chronology of events—no need to go into great detail, just record the facts. Then answer the questions, *Where does it happen? When does it happen? How does it happen? Who makes it happen? What are their relationships to each other? What is it that motivates them?*

The form of the play will also determine things about your character. Is it comic or serious? Is it representational or presentational? (See chapter 6.) Is it realistic or abstract? Is it a short sketch or a longer play?

Understanding the style of the piece will allow you to set boundaries for your character. A short sketch, or a piece that is comic, presentational, or abstract may allow, or, even call for, a broader character, while a serious, realistic drama has more defined expectations for its characters.

The character will be a primary focus in your study of the text. Character analysis is a lot like detective work. You investigate clues, ask questions, and draw conclusions. Some details are evident from the lines in the script, while others will be hidden beneath the surface and require some deduction. Some questions will not have a ready answer. It will be up to you to fill in the blanks. This exploration can be fun and fascinating.

Some questions to ask about your character as you start your analysis are:

What do I say about myself? (Is it true?) *What do the other characters say about me?* (Is that true?) *How old am I? Do I act my age? What are my physical characteristics? Do I have any physical limitations? Where do I come from? What is my education? What is my social/economic standing? What is my family like?* (It can be fun to create a family history, but don't get bogged down in this. Your focus is the time frame of the play.) *What has happened before the play begins that will have an affect on my character during the course of the play?*

Next ask questions that will take you deeper, so that you can better understand your character's primary motivations in the play. Ask the questions, *What do I hope for or dream about? What obstacles stand in my way? What would I fight for? What are my values; what do I believe? Do I mean what I say? Do I say what I mean? How do I feel about each of the other characters? What do I discover in the course of the play? How do I change in the course of the play? Where do I invest strong emotion? What surprises me? What brings me joy? What makes me laugh? What makes me sad?*

As you build a character, remember that, whether that character is evil or good, as an actor you must approach them by *understanding* what motivates them, not by *judging* their behavior as right or wrong.

Evil people rarely see themselves as evil. If you are to play such a character well, focus on what it is that they want and what they love. They, the character, must not be an enemy to you, the actor. Let it be the audience that passes judgment on the character's motives and actions.

After you have answered the above questions, you should have a pretty clear picture of your character. Next, you want to look for the elements in yourself that you can select to best portray the character: *How are you like the character? What have you experienced that will help you understand the experiences of the character? Can you identify with the character's feelings, moods, aspirations, or relationships?*

Some actors like to keep a journal as their character. Some write letters as their character to other characters in the play. This may help you understand your character better and make choices with confidence.

Research. With some scripts, you may need to do a little research. If the play is set in a time period or location that is unfamiliar, it is worth your time to do some study. Histories, picture books, maps, and films can all help give you the understanding you need. The time and place may affect the way the character speaks and moves, the way they carry themselves, and even the way they think. If you are playing a historical figure you will want to know as much as you can about them. A good library is the first place to go for information on your subject.

If you are to portray someone from a generation or two ago, talk to a relative or family friend of that age. They can offer invaluable insights—insights you may never find in written histories—into customs, manners, expressions, and the like. Also, make sure you know both the meaning and the pronunciation of any unfamiliar words in the script.

Humor is an important element to understand in developing a character.

Shedding a Little "Light"

Humor is an important element in any form of theater. A sense of humor in a character is captivating. It can win an audience's heart and hold their attention. Explore where you may find humor in any character you play. They may have a subtle wit or a slapstick physical comedy. They may be a merry joker or someone unaware of how funny they are. Incongruity—the unexpected, the surprise—is quite often the key for humor.

Let's take the story of Cinderella, for example. Each of

the characters are well-known—the two jealous and cruel stepsisters, the evil stepmother, the loving fairy godmother, the prince. But imagine if:

- Cinderella has a slight cold or a sneeze
- One of the stepsisters has an obnoxious giggle
- The stepmother has a slight lisp
- The other stepsister is always tripping over her skirt
- The fairy godmother knocks things over with her wand
- The prince snorts when he laughs

Humor can bring a fresh perspective to an old story. Even in small doses it can make a character brighter and more memorable.

While we're on the subject of humor, we should make note of the art of laughter for the actor. Laughing naturally on stage is a special skill. It takes relaxation and good breath support. Practice different laughs—a nasal snicker, a high-pitched giggle, a raucous guffaw. Everyone laughs in their own way. Find an interesting laugh for your character. Remember, it should be natural and one that you are comfortable with—a true laugh can bring more humanity to your acting.

When Words are Enough

In some sketches or readings it may not be appropriate or necessary for you to create a character. The idea or the words in the piece are the focus. In a dramatic reading of poetry or Scripture the actor brings an energy and vitality to the words. Vocal control, texture, and emotional color are the important elements. The audience is engaged by the words or the ideas, not by a character.

Rehearsals: Time To Explore

Rehearsal can be a great time of exploration. It is the actor's task to take the information in the script and combine it with the director's concept and his own imagination, observation, and experience to build a distinctive, believable character. After the initial script study, most of this work will take place in rehearsals.

The actor's responsibility in rehearsal is to be attentive, cooperative, supportive, and enjoyable. Individual directors will have differing methods and structures for rehearsals. As an actor, you need to remain flexible and be ready to jump in when needed.

Rehearsal is where the play begins to find its life. It is a collaborative effort between director, playwright, and actors, each bringing their ideas and energies together. If the atmosphere of rehearsals is relaxed and joyful with the excitement of the work at hand, and the company is looking forward to the performance to come, look for wonderful things to happen!

Rehearsal Guidelines for the Actor:

DOs

- Show respect for your fellow actors by always being on time.
- Do your homework before you get to rehearsal.
- Know your lines, and be off script by the time agreed upon.
- Review your blocking (stage movement) on your own.
- Come with ideas for your character.
- Experiment—try both the outrageous and the subtle.
- Arrive ten to fifteen minutes early to warm-up physically and vocally.

- Encourage your fellow actors.
- Leave any frustrations of the day outside the rehearsal door.
- Spend your extra time memorizing lines.

DON'Ts

- Don't direct other actors. If you have an idea about concept, blocking, or someone else's character, tell the director, not the other actor.
- Don't invite anyone to rehearsal without getting the director's approval. Spectators can be a distraction.
- Don't talk when you are not rehearsing. Step outside or into another room if you need to talk.
- Don't comment on your costume to anyone but the director or costumer.
- Don't wait for the performance to give your best!

Treat the time and the people around you with care and respect, and you'll find rehearsals to be very satisfying.

Very important work takes place in rehearsals. Although much of this will be the responsibility of the director, the actor is not a pawn on a chess board. Your creative input is essential. Here are some areas where you will want to contribute in rehearsals:

Memorization. Rehearsal is where you will normally finish learning your lines. Beginning actors are often frightened by the idea of memorization. For some people it can be a problem. Your memory is like a muscle: the more it is exercised, the better it will work. It needs the attention of a calm and focused mind.

Actors approach memorization individually.

- Some actors memorize by first gaining the idea or sense of what their lines mean. They then put their lines into their own words and, a bit at a time, learn the specific words of the script.

- Some find that they learn best by rote, repeating the line out loud, over and over until they own it.

- Some memorize by repeatedly writing out their lines in longhand.

- Some use a tape recorder, recording their lines and cues, and play it over and over. Then they tape only the other character's lines leaving enough of a pause to speak their lines aloud.

- Some have a friend or spouse speak the other characters' lines while watching the actor's lines to correct any mistakes.

Use whichever method works best for you.

Blocking. In rehearsal, the director will tell you where they want you to move on the stage. This is referred to as *blocking.* Some directors will give you very detailed blocking; others will leave much of the movement up to you. In either case, any move you make on stage should have impulse or reason behind it. It is your job to motivate (find the reason for) the movement. If there is no motivation, your movement will seem awkward and without meaning. Move with a purpose from one place to another and you will bring energy and life to your performance. Be selective. Constant movement may be distracting. Don't be afraid to stand still.

Entrances and Exits. Your character has an *offstage* life as well as the *onstage* life that the audience sees. Understanding this offstage life can make your performance more complete. To help with this, ask yourself these questions before you enter or exit the stage:

- Where am I coming from as I step on the stage?
- Did I intend to stay or was I passing through to another place?

- What have I been doing?
- Where am I going when I leave?
- How do I feel about where I am going?

The answers to these questions might be found in the script, be given to you by the director, or come from your imagination. Whatever the source, they can help provide motivation and focus.

Listening. One of the most important skills an actor can develop is how to listen on stage. Skilled listening offers a sharper focus for fellow actors and makes your responses more believable. Beginning actors click off and on. When another actor is speaking they are blank, as if their "hold" button was punched. When it is their turn to speak, they suddenly come to life! Practice listening. Whether you are looking at the actor speaking or not, your character has an attitude or a response to what is being said.

Cues. Slow cue pickups is a common mistake in acting. A cue is the last phrase or word spoken by another actor prior to your line. Many actors fall into a habit of hearing their cue and then taking a beat to breathe or react before speaking their line. This sets up a rhythm that is not only unnatural, but can lull an audience to sleep! Unless the director has asked for a pause between your cue and your line, do not put one in yourself. React to the other actor's line while he is speaking, and speak immediately after him. In dialogue there are most often words which spark the thought of your next line. These words will help you keep on top of your cues.

Pace. Your job when speaking is to move the action of the play forward. Many actors fall into the trap of thinking that every word is important—or at least speak like they are. They emphasize almost every word in a sentence. This unnatural pattern not only slows down the pace of the play, but, after time, the audience no longer understands what is being said! Instead, speak clearly but swiftly through to the end of your sentences. Choose only one word in the sentence that should be stressed.

It is possible to speak too rapidly, but the more common mistake is to speak too slowly. A clear, bright pace will strengthen your communication.

Discoveries. There will be times in the script when your character makes a discovery. It may be a new thought or sudden realization that he makes; or, it may be information given to him by someone else. Whenever your character makes a discovery, allow the audience to make the discovery with you. Keep it fresh. Avoid simply reporting your lines. Let them see the thought come to you as you say it. This spontaneity of a fresh, first-time response draws your audience into the discovery.

Opposites. As you work on your character, you will develop ideas about how you should speak a line and how the character feels at any given moment. Be careful not to make immediate and obvious decisions. Often, playing against the emotion or intention is more interesting. We often fight to hide our emotions, because we "should" or we don't want people to see what we are really feeling. The fight to hide our emotions can produce a fascinating energy.

Let's say, for example, that your character is angry. The obvious choice is to talk loudly or yell. Instead, try playing against the emotion. The character may fight not to show his anger by lowering his voice and speaking very distinctly.

Or our character may be sad and emotional. The obvious choice is to cry and moan or to whine. Instead, play the opposite, and mix the tears with laughter. Many times the obvious or first choice is the one you will want to keep. But remember to explore other options before you settle on one.

Rehearsal is the place to explore, discover, and refine. It should be an exciting time of building and polishing your character. By the last rehearsal, you should feel confident and ready to step into performance.

Performance: Giving Gifts

The performance is where the final character—the audience—is added to your play. Without an audience there is no real theater, only literature and experimentation. The audience completes your presentation. As an actor before an audience, you will discover things about your character and about timing that you were unaware of in rehearsal. In performance, all your work finds its focus.

Don't look at performances as a chance for people to come and see *you*. Rather, offer your performance as a gift to *them*. You have characters you want them to meet, emotions you want them to feel, and ideas you want them to consider. Give them out as gifts.

It goes without saying that you will always be on time for any performance. The stage manager or director will set a *call time* when all the cast should be at the performance site. Give yourself plenty of time to warm up and to get into costume and makeup if it is called for.

We like to plan a brief time of prayer before all our performances. If you do this, schedule it so that the actors have the time they need for any last-minute preparation.

We find it helpful, no matter if we are performing a short sketch or a two-hour play, for an actor to take a few minutes alone to focus her thoughts on the task ahead. No matter what pre-performance routine you settle on, be respectful of other actors' time and space.

Performance presents its own set of challenges to an actor. Here are a few tips:

Stage Fright. The fear that seizes every actor from time to time is normal. A recent survey of adults found that their greatest fear was speaking before an audience. Acting is vulnerable work; you are putting yourself on the line. But remember, you have the support of fellow actors, and you have prepared well. The audience is not sitting in judgment; they want to like you. Don't listen to the voices that say *I can't do this.* Tell yourself *I can!* Focus that nervous energy you feel. Harness it; take it out onstage and have it work *for* you.

Play the Moment. One of the major challenges for a beginning actor is to *play the moment.* Don't get ahead of yourself. Don't think of the entire performance. Take it line by line, response by response. Listen (*really* hear) your fellow actors. Don't act as if you know what happens at the end—play the moment you are in.

Take, for example, Shakespeare's *Romeo and Juliet.* Two families are at odds with each other. The couple—a boy from one and a girl from the other—falls in love, but the families continue to quarrel. Misunderstandings and murders follow. Life is complicated for the young lovers and not long after their marriage they also die. It's a sad story. But what makes us feel sorrow is not just their death. It is the twists and the surprises in the story. It is death contrasted to their love and the vitality of their lives. The actors playing Romeo and Juliet must not act as if they know they are going to die! They must play their care and love of life. They must play the moment, forgetting the end. That way their deaths shock and hurt us—even though *we* know how the story ends.

Breaking Character. Occasionally something will happen onstage that is a complete surprise and will seem very funny. You may want to laugh. If the sketch or play is realistic, don't! It may seem impossible to control yourself. Try. Try very hard. If you "break character," you break the illusion of reality. The audience will suddenly feel uncomfortable. If you play through any surprise situation "in-character" the audience will believe you.

Covering. Anything can happen on stage—a line is dropped, someone forgets an entrance, or one of your props is missing. Don't panic. If you have done your homework and are relaxed, your mind will find a way out. Keep the play moving—ad lib to keep the story on track. This is where ensemble playing makes a difference. Trust your fellow actors and yourself. Respond as your character would to the situation. Above all, support your fellow actor. Don't give up or say *I'm sorry* in the middle of a performance! If you commit and push through, the audience will never know it wasn't planned from the first.

Consistency. Your character may change slightly in performance, due to timing and audience response. But it is important to keep the character you developed in rehearsal. Remember that acting is collaboration. Your fellow actors are depending on you. Don't surprise them. Clear any changes with the director or stage manager and inform the other actors before the performance. Be consistent and you will win the respect of your fellow actors. If you are performing the same piece many times, remember that even though it's the tenth time you've performed the play, it's the audience's first time to see it!

Imagination. Albert Einstein once said, "Imagination is more important than knowledge." This great man realized that mere facts, mere information, was empty without the perspective of imagination to see the possibilities, to imagine what could be. Our imagination is one of the Creator's most exciting gifts. Yet, sadly, it is a gift whose use and development is no longer encouraged by our culture. It is a gift that is forgotten as we grow older.

A recent study showed that 95 percent of the mental process of a child of four involved the imagination; by the time that child reaches thirteen, it will have dropped to 40 percent and by the time most of us have reached thirty, the use of our imagination is down to only 4 percent of our thought process.

Today if imagination is encouraged at all it is most often self-serving and narcissistic. It has lost its grounding in the truth and in a vision for a higher good. Today we are encouraged merely to exercise our fantasies.

The use of imagination in the mental process drops from 95 percent to 4 percent by the time we reach thirty!

As an actor you have the amazing opportunity to exercise your imagination, and to call an audience to exercise theirs. Acting is a disciplined craft, but it is also imagination at play. Remember that we have only to look at God's abundant Creation to witness the value that he places on imagination. Use the gifts and the opportunities you are given to serve our creative Lord!

8
Costumes

"Clothes make the man" someone once said. Well, philosophically, I can't agree. On the stage, however . . . that's another story. What an actor wears tells us a great deal about the character he portrays. In the theater a costume definitely helps to "make the man."

An audience builds its emotional and intellectual response on what they hear an actor say, and what they see an actor do, but what an actor wears greatly impacts the viewer's initial reaction to the character. An actor's clothing also helps to set the time, place, mood, and perspective of the presentation.

Enter the Costumer

If you've been given the title, *costume designer* (what we'll call the *costumer*), or if you're responsible for finding someone to be in charge of the costumes, then this chapter is for you.

What follows is an overview of the costumer's responsibilities for a full-scale drama production. But remember, each production is unique. Not all of them will require every step outlined here. However, if you understand how to approach the costuming for a larger production, you will find the task even easier for a smaller one.

First of all, bear in mind that being the person responsible for the costumes doesn't mean you have to be able to sew, but it does help! What's most important is your creative imagination—the ability to visualize something before it exists. It also helps if you are:

Aware—of how line, color and texture work together

Organized—in ordering your time, and in directing a sewing crew when necessary

Resourceful—knowing how to find the information you will need, and willing to ask for help

Thrifty—an avid hunter in thrift stores, bargain basements, and friend's closets

Enthusiastic—blessed with an abundance of stamina

This describes some of the characteristics required of a costumer, now let's look at what the costumer must actually do.

Concepts

First, read the script. If possible, read it before you meet with the director. That way you'll have some understanding of his discussion about the characters, and the overall feeling, mood, or theme of the piece.

The director's concept for the production may include specific costume needs, or it may not. As the costumer you will discuss with the director ideas for style, line, color, and fabric choices. The director makes sure that all the production elements fit together consistently, and convey the concept you have agreed upon. You design the costumes within the framework of the director's concept. A director may want very little input in the design, or a great deal, depending on his experience and directing style. Determine if he has strong initial feelings about color, texture, or style.

Actors portray a barnyard of animals for our adaptation of *The Book of the Dun Cow*. Costume design by Mike Buckley and Veronica Smith. (LPT 1988)

Early on, you'll also want to confer with the set and lighting designers to discuss your ideas and determine any overlapping elements. (For example, the set may need to be designed openly enough to allow women in period hoop skirts.)

In determining design, remember to ask these questions:

- ***Schedule.*** When are the production dates? How much time do you have to put the costumes together? How often will the production be performed? The answer to this may determine how well-made the costumes need to be.

- ***Audience.*** If it's to be a children's theater or a street theater audience, you'll want more color, more "splash" to grab and hold their attention. If it's a performance before a regular Sunday church service, the costuming may be very simple.

- ***Space Considerations.*** If the audience is small and in close proximity to the performers, the details of a costume are more critical.

- ***Casting Considerations.*** What is the size of the cast? What are the body types and sizes?

- ***Budget.*** What monetary resources are available? If you have a large reserve, that's great! If not, crank up your imagination. Amazing things can be done with pieces "found and borrowed."

- ***Characters.*** Are they gentle, mysterious, loud, sultry, or conservative? Do you want the audience to draw firm conclusions about specific characters' personalities? Costuming can play a large role in this area.

Note: It's important to record all your decisions. It's surprising how easy it is to forget details. This way you may also avoid possible misunderstandings with crew members later.

Impressions

Now your work really begins. Read the script again with a pad and pencil at your side. Make notes about the characters. Jot down how they make you feel and any images that come to you. Make a note of everything that might affect your design choices. Some particulars to settle:

- ***Time.*** Is the period 1863 or 1946—futuristic, timeless . . . ? What season of the year—winter, summer . . . ? Is it early morning, mid-afternoon, twilight?

- ***Location.*** Europe or Asia? Mountain or desert? What's the climate, . . . the weather? Is the action taking place indoors or out?

- ***Occupations of the Characters.*** Farmer, doctor, homemaker or bank executive? What are their social standings? Rich, poor? Educated, or unschooled?

- ***Age and Relationships.*** Very old or young? Family members? Co-workers? Rivals—friends?

- ***Scenes.*** Ball games? Picnics? The workplace?

- ***Miscellaneous.*** Are costume changes necessary? How much time is needed? Will any costume get wet, muddied or torn?

Note: Make sure you reread the script a number of times. It's surprising how many new details you discover on each new reading.

Research

It is often necessary to do a certain amount of research. None of us knows everything about everything. And the director is busy with other things. He counts on you for accuracy and consistency with the costuming.

Reference Books. If the the production is set in another time period, the best place to start is the library. There is often a large selection in the reference section covering costumes through the ages. (Some of these are listed under our "Further Reading" section on page 257.) For costumes of the nineteenth century and earlier, look for paintings in both books and museums. Remember, however, that the majority of portraits were of the wealthy.

Periodicals. For twentieth-century styles, magazines are a handy reference. Most libraries have past issues of *Life*, *Post*, and *McCalls*. In addition, many have the fashion magazines like *Vogue* and *Harpers Bazaar*. Pay attention to advertisements as well as feature photos.

Catalogs. An old Sears Roebuck catalog is invaluable if you can find the right year. There are reproductions of some issues available at the library. They contain photos or drawings of all manner of clothing for all ages, from hats and gloves right down to underwear.

Today's mail-order catalogs are also helpful when designing a contemporary production. Some catalogs will even give you the flavor of a specific geographical area, such as New England or the Pacific Northwest. Catalogs are also useful for specific purchases, such as military uniforms, dancewear, and custom T-shirts.

Film and Video. Films are a great research tool, especially now that they are available on video. Films and older TV series that are set in the decade in which they are filmed are generally accurate. (However, don't mistake every film as historically accurate. Many times the interpretation of historical styles are influenced by the styles of the year in which a film was made!)

Personal Resources. Don't forget your own family archives. Family photo albums can be a surprising resource. We had great fun with our annual *Festival of Christmas* the

Molly McMurry and Kurt Reichert take part in a real family Christmas in the 1950s Midwest. (*Festival of Christmas*, 1988. Costume design by Veronica Smith.)

year it was about a midwestern family in 1952. Our costumer, Vicki, needed to dress three generations—small children, a teenager, adult children, and grandparents. She looked through her own mid-western family photos from the fifties and found everything she needed. She even designed the little girls' dresses after a dress she remembered wearing as a child.

Observation. For contemporary pieces, the world around you is your best research tool. For a show about teenagers, spend an afternoon on a high-school campus (first check in at the office!). Be aware of everyone you see and make mental notes of how they look—the mechanic who fixes your car, your neighbor, the clerk in the department store, the elderly woman who crosses the street in front of your car. Don't get impatient; use the time to study her clothing. What type of shoes is she wearing—are they worn, polished? Look at the color of her stockings—do they fit or bag at the ankles? Is her hem straight? Does her slip show? What color is her dress—print or solid? What is the fabric? Does she have a sweater on—does it match? Is she wearing a scarf or a hat—what type of jewelry? You can learn much just by taking the time to observe the world around you.

The Design: Line, Color, and Texture

Now you're ready to start your design. You'll pull together everything from your meeting with the director, your impressions from the script, your research, and your own imagination. Keep in mind that you are part of a whole. You are working in collaboration with others. Talk often with the set and lighting designers to ensure a unity of design. The right combination of line, color, and texture in your design not only creates visual interest, but gives the audience clues to the characters themselves.

Line. Put someone tall and thin in vertical stripes and he'll seem even taller and lankier. Want a character to be more comical? Try making his pants too short. Line gives an audience information in subtle ways. The lines you have to work with are not only in patterns on the fabric but in the garment itself: neckline, hemline, waistline, sleeve length and shape, shape of the bodice, drape of skirt, pants, even the cut of shoulders—a round or scalloped neckline will give a softer feeling to a character than a more severe square or V-neck.

The way in which a character's costume moves speaks silently to the audience. Is the drape full and free or tight and restrictive? With the line of the costumes you could help contrast one character's softness and ease, with the awkward stiffness of another.

Color. Color can help set a mood, add important splash, or highlight contrast. You can help keep your design cohesive by selecting a color theme—earth tones, primary colors, metallic, black and white, and so on.

Some colors are more flattering than others for any given actor. Choose your colors carefully. Experiment. Remember to consult with the set designer. You don't want the actors to fade into the set or clash with it unwittingly. (Try using richer or deeper shades of the same or complimentary colors to those of the set.) In any case, you don't want to annoy audiences with opposing color themes.

People often associate color with attitudes, feelings, or mood. Bright colors can be happy or powerful. Dark colors can be somber or mysterious. Earth tones, like green, warm gold and soft browns, can give a sense of comfort, safety, or gentleness of spirit. Cool colors, like blue, grey, and black, can give the feeling of cold, emptiness or rigidity. Hot colors, like red, orange, bright yellow, can exude vibrancy, anger, or surprise.

Texture. You can enhance the personality of a character, as well as add visual interest or contrast, with texture. Often, the heavier the texture the more earthy the character will appear. The finer the weave, the more pristine. The silks and brocades of royalty offer sharp contrast to the hand woven woolens of a peasant. The character of an old Gypsy woman in layers of handspun cotton, wool, tapestry and leather presents a lot more interest than if the fabric is all of the same texture. The following provide examples:

- In our readers theater productions, the primary focus is the script—the literature. So, we costume the performers in outfits that are pleasant, but will not draw attention to themselves, e.g., clean lines, soft colors, and smooth texture.

- Our production of *The Diviners* was set in rural America during the depression. The director wanted the feeling of an old patchwork quilt. Our costumes were of soft lines, in a wide variety of colors, all rather faded and worn.

- Our street theater production, *The Quest of Everyman,* is a contemporary comedy set in medieval style. The costuming carries bright splashes of color, big and bold, which help attract attention.

- In our production of *St. Joan*, not only was everyone in modern dress, but the character of Joan was the only one in color. The director wanted her faith and courage to stand out against the men of politics and religion. So we costumed all the men in shades of brown, like an old sepia photograph—whether they were soldiers, bishops, cardinals or kings.

If you will be constructing your own costumes, you will need to take these additional steps:

Sketching. By sketching out the costume ideas for each character, you start to translate your mental images into solid form. Working only with pencil and paper, this is a time to play. Experiment with different choices of line and style.

Remember your job is to enhance the character, not to have a fashion show. Don't be afraid to try some unexpected choices. (We set our production of Shakespeare's *Much Ado About Nothing* in the American Southwest of the 1860s. We costumed the money-hungry Borachio as a very stylish gambler instead of a scruffy bad guy. He stood in contrast to his companion in crime, Don John, who we dressed as a trapper in dirty buckskins!)

The trio of scoundrels (left); Aloysius Mullally as Don John, Tim Tulumello as Borachio and Bill Barstad as Conrad In *Much Ado About Nothing* (LPT 1989). Right, Deborah Gilmour Smyth, *Saint Joan*. Costume designs by Veronica Smith. (LPT 1988)

Swatching. Gathering fabric samples, called swatches, can be a great help in your selection of color and texture. Most fabric stores will be glad to cut swatches for you and some will even let you cut your own. Take an envelope for each store where you'll be shopping, so you'll know where you found various fabrics. Be sure to note the price of each selection on the back of the swatch. (This can sometimes make a difficult choice easier if you have a small budget.) Don't only swatch pieces you know you're going to use. Give yourself lots of options. A certain fabric might look better in the store than it does when put with other colors, designs, and textures you've already chosen and vice versa.

Notice, not only color and pattern, but texture and content of the fabric. Remember:

- Polyester double knit looks like polyester double knit. It is a late twentieth-century fabric and if the audience is close to the actors, it won't do for period costumes.

- Synthetics are easy to launder, and they wear like iron. They are especially useful in productions that are highly physical, have many costume changes, or will be performed over a long period of time.

- Cotton (preferably 100 percent) is also easily laundered, though often needs ironing. It doesn't promote perspiration as much as synthetics. It's excellent for shirts and bodices.

- Other natural fibers, such as woolens, linens, silks, and blends, offer a wide variety of texture. They are generally more expensive and need to be dry cleaned. (Remember your budget.) They are great for skirts and pants and can be used more economically for accent pieces, such as vests and shawls, that don't require as much yardage but will give a nice variety in texture.

Renderings. Once you have settled on the fabrics you will use, it is helpful to draw color renderings. A color rendering is an illustration that clearly communicates to the director and the other designers how each costume will look. Attach your fabric swatches to the rendering. This assures that you are communicating what you think you are communicating.

A director might say he wants a skirt flared. Does he mean A-line, circle, or gored? If he wants a cowboy hat for a character, does he mean a ten-gallon or Stetson? Renderings help clarify all this. It is also helpful for anyone who might be assisting you in building or shopping for the costumes.

If renderings are out of the question due to time, inability to draw well, or other hindrances, catalogs or magazines can help. Designs can be illustrated by mounting

Cut and paste "renderings" help communicate to the director and stitchers. The finished product is what counts. Hero and Beatrice in LP production of *Much Ado About Nothing*.

photographs on separate pieces of paper according to character. Another option is to make copies of the pictures on a pattern envelope, or copy drawings from books and attach the corresponding fabric swatches so the director can see exactly what you're hoping to create.

Go over each character's rendering with the director. Clarify anything that seems unclear or vague and, above all, be flexible and willing to make changes. The director has final say over everything.

Costume Plot. Once the director has approved your designs, your next step is to make a costume plot. List each character and every costume piece they need right down to shoes and socks. Don't forget to include items like eyeglasses, jewelry, gloves, and so on. It's these small details that help us believe this is a real person. Don't forget special undergarments like corsets and petticoats for period shows.

Rendering by Michael Buckley for *The Book of the Dun Cow* takes Chauntecleer the Rooster from the reality of the page to the fantasy of the stage.

When the designs are approved by the director, you are ready to start making it all come true. This is where your costume designs take form and become reality. This can be accomplished in many ways. You can build them yourself, or you can rent, buy, or borrow them.

Building. If you're going to build the costumes you'll need a crew of seamstresses. (Or this may be you!) If they can draft patterns—terrific! But pattern drafting is not a necessity. There are companies who sell patterns for period clothing (listed in the back) and contemporary patterns can be modified into many sizes and styles by an experienced seamstress. There are also books with pattern graphs for both men's and women's period clothing. Don't be intimidated by them. It's not as difficult as it might seem. If you have a head for logic, it can even be fun.

You've kept your swatches, so shopping for the fabric will be quite simple. Use your pattern or pattern book fabric charts, for amounts of yardage to purchase. You might use one seamstress as your right hand, working closely with you on the cutting, and several other volunteers to do the actual sewing.

Volunteer stitchers are more than worth their weight in gold! Establish a core group and learn their strengths and weaknesses, likes and dislikes. Give complicated projects to the more experienced. There may be someone who doesn't have a sewing machine but would love to do handwork, such as hems, embroidery, lace, or buttons.

Keep track of *who* has what project and *when* it's scheduled to be complete. Give them reasonable deadlines and make sure they understand the importance of sticking to them. Encourage them to ask if there's something that's unclear. Make yourself available by phone at all hours of day or night for their questions. (You'll avoid costly mistakes, extra man hours, and ruined fabric.) Praise them. And thank them a lot.

Left: Rented WWI uniform and borrowed authentic highland garb enhance history and heritage. David Heath and Chris Cederberg in *Kilts*. (LPT 1988) Right: This dress was solid white when rented, all trim and lace was added. Cynthia Peters in *Amadeus*. Costume designs by Veronica Smith (LPT 1989).

Renting. Local professional and community theaters very often rent out costumes from their costume stock. Universities and colleges with large theater departments usually do the same. There are also costume houses in most major cities. They are especially good resources for period military uniforms and exotic costumes. After you have developed a working relationship, and having rented from them several times, ask if they will give you a professional discount rate. Don't expect it, but it doesn't hurt to ask. Most costume shops require a substantial deposit, but will usually take a check to hold until the items are returned.

When renting, be specific about what you need as far as period, style, color, and sizes. They might not have exactly what you want, so be creative. Perhaps a garment of a different color will work as well. Maybe a dress would be suitable if you could add some trim. Be sure to find out if they allow alterations for fit or modifications for style and color. Most shops do, but you will usually need to return it to its original condition before bringing it back.

Rental costumes are worn by many people and often need repair. In the case of theaters or schools, costume rental is a sideline, not their business. They don't generally do repairs, but are usually most happy to have you repair a garment you're interested in renting. Don't expect the fee to be discounted. If you want it badly enough, be glad you found it in the correct size and repair it with a smile. It goes without saying that garments should be returned laundered or dry cleaned and in good repair.

If something unforeseen happens to a rented costume (e.g., an actor brushes up against wet paint), contact the rental shop immediately to make appropriate recompense.

Shopping to Buy. Buying new costumes can be expensive. But it may be the option for you depending on your budget, time, and personnel. It may be an unavoidable option when it is critical that the production's costumes be up to the minute in fashion. Shop discount outlets where you can find quality garments and name brand labels for big savings.

One way to help defray your costs on new purchases, is to sell them to the actor at a reduced rate. If he is interested, offer him the item at the end of the production's run. Half price is fair.

Thrifting. You and your local thrift stores will become good friends. The thrifts are great places to find shoes, hats, men's suits, and all types of clothing from the last twenty years. (It's relatively easy to modify the lapels of a man's suit to the higher buttoning, smaller lapels of the Victorian era.) Occasionally you'll find a gem from the thirties, forties, or fifties. Again, remember that all your characters are not fashion plates. It would be natural for some to be wearing styles from ten or fifteen years earlier.

Left: All the costume pieces were purchased at thrift stores. Rick Meads and Stacey Allen in *The Foreigner.* (LPT 1988) Right: All the costumes for *I am the Brother of Dragons* were purchased new because an up-to-the-minute look was important in communicating to teen-age audiences. Chris Causey, Janine Zeller, Mike Gier, Anna Carminito. Costume designs by Veronica Smith. (LPT 1987)

Keep your eyes open for vintage clothing shops. They are usually set up more like a fine dress shop and stock high quality used clothing from the 1920s to 1960s. They often have authentic period accessories as well. Be warned, their prices are much higher than the thrift stores.

You say you've got a large goose egg in the column next to "costume budget"? Well, don't despair. Use your imagination. It is still wise to have a costume designer. This will give unity to the costumes and ultimately to the production.

Ask your actors. They have clothes in their closets and best of all, they're probably the correct size. Talk to them about your color themes and desired styles. If they are willing to use their own clothes, ask them to bring in several things to compare. You may even find cast members who are willing to buy a costume piece for themselves.

If you are designing a period show, pulling from closets is not so easy. Ask the extended families. Maybe there is an old dress that Aunt Jenny has from 1928. Perhaps Grandad's World War II uniform is too small for his six foot grandson, but might fit a smaller actor who just happens to need a vintage uniform.

Put a notice in your church bulletin. List what you need and ask people to check through their closets. Be prepared to sift through lots of unusable clothing. You'd be amazed what people come up with. But who knows, it may be just the thing. Look beyond the surface. Replacing the trim on a shirt, adding a flounce to a dress, or reshaping the sleeves, could be all it needs.

Vintage clothing shops have been the source of costumes for many productions of our annual *Festival of Christmas*. Carolyn Schade, Vanda Eggington, Mike Buckley, Mark Crouse on left in 1985 (designed by Margaret Neuhoff Vida) and Teres Byrne and Greg Adams on right in 1988 (designed by Veronica Smith).

It's not out of the question to ask actors to supply their own costumes for period productions. But make sure they understand this from the first. After the appropriate research, the costumer can make a packet for each actor that contains good detailed pictures of clothing from the period, depending on their character type. Include fabric swatches or suggestions that they can use as guidelines. Remind them to be true to their character in their choices. (A cobbler would dress quite differently than a banker. A respectable woman would not be seen in red in the 1860s.) Include the local rental sources you know of and sources for period patterns. The actor now has the option of making his own costume, having it made, or renting. Make sure they all understand that you, the costumer, are responsible for the unity of the costumes and have power of veto. If they are going to have the costume made, you need to approve designs and swatches.

The annual Christmas production of *Carols by Candlelight* at San Diego's First Assembly of God, has each actor provide their own costume.

Stock and Storage. Once you start accumulating costume pieces, either from building, buying, or receiving donations, you'll need a place to store them. Perhaps an unused room or closet at the church or a volunteer's home. Depending on the climate in your area, avoid basements or garages. If they tend to be damp in your area the clothing, especially shoes, will mildew.

The wonderful thing about developing your own costume stock is that you can draw from it for future projects.

Another plus to having your own costume stock is the ability to *distress* them when needed. Distressing makes a costume look lived-in, i.e., faded, dirty, and so on. Think about it—a farmer working in the field all day wouldn't be in a brand new pair of overalls with a newly pressed shirt! The overalls would be faded (bleach or fade-out works) and well-worn in front, along pockets, on the knees and seat. (A metal food grater or sand paper does a nice job.) For the dirty look, fabric paints and diluted liquid dyes work well. Their advantage over real dirt, is that they don't wash out. You can also use white cream shoe polish for faded spots and brown or black for dirt, but they come out when laundered.

Costume Parade

Scheduling a costume parade a few days before the first dress rehearsal is a handy way to plan any last-minute corrections or changes. It is amazing how a costume changes when it comes off the hanger and on to the body it was designed for.

At a costume parade, the director and costumer look at the characters one-by-one and note any changes needed. A hem may be either too short or too long, a blouse may need some decorative trim, seams may need to be taken in or let out. A suit needs a different tie, a dress needs to be worn with a pendant instead of pearls. The costume parade allows you more time for these adjustments than if you wait until the first dress rehearsal.

Costume parades also give the director and costumer a picture of how characters look together. The costumer can see how colors work next to each other, if couples look good together, or whether a costume needs a shawl or a different belt. The costumer also attends dress rehearsals to see how things look in performance, how quick changes are working, and how the costumes move.

Maintenance

Once the show opens you may be responsible for laundry and maintenance of the costumes. But by this time most costumers are ready for a trip to Hawaii (or at least a day at the park)! So, often this responsibility is delegated to a volunteer or cast member. Make sure the person assigned understands:

- what can and cannot be laundered
- what needs to be hand washed
- what should not be put in the dryer
- any other secrets about the care of a garment

It is also a good idea that all costume pieces, even those that belong to the actor, are kept in one place. It's too easy for an actor to forget to bring back his shoes or his shirt in his rush to get to the performance.

Obviously all the productions you do will not be on a large scale. Often they may be a simple sketch or a readers theater piece. However, what the performers wear is still important. They don't need to look as if they were cut from the same cookie cutter, but it gives a clean, focused look when colors and styles are coordinated. Use colors that flatter each individual performer, and that blend with the others. You can tie them together with a common thread of color, tone, or accessory. The planned combination of simple street clothing can suggest things about the characters that help them come to life for the audience.

Left, coordinated street clothes work well for our touring production *Take Joy*. (Designed by Kristen Allen.) Right, wild costumes add a fun flavor to *Say No, Max*, a production on drug abuse for elementary students. (Designed by Margaret Neuhoff Vida.)

The versatility of story theater can be enhanced by using props and single costume pieces (hat, shawl, apron, vest). An actor can change from character to character in the blink of an eye, while the imagination of the audience completes the picture.

Make sure one actor's clothes don't overpower the others, unless his character should stand out.

Special Effects

This section could be titled, "What to Do When the Director Asks the Impossible!" Sometimes a director or playwright asks the costumer to work miracles. They are sure it is easy to make adults look like children, women look like men, men look like roosters, and even give a waist to someone whom God didn't see clear to give one! Amazingly enough, most of this isn't that difficult to achieve—with a few tricks.

The right costume can turn adults into kids...left, Deborah Gilmour Smyth and Tad Buffington in *You're a Good Man, Charlie Brown* (design by Gail Parish, LPT 1980)...OR, make a young woman old...right, Deborah Gilmour Smyth in *Waking Dreams* (design by Margaret Neuhoff Vida, LPT 1985).

With good makeup and some well-placed padding, a young man becomes a portly gentleman, a young woman becomes a matronly aunt, a thin actress is instantly pregnant. Polyester batting is your best bet for padding, but proceed with caution. If you want it to look natural, don't overdo age, makeup, or padding. A little goes a long way!

Give an adult a youthful hairstyle and a costume with little shape that seems one size too large, and you can give the illusion of a child.

Shave a woman's head, bind her chest, dress her in masculine garments, give her shoes that are too big and voila!

Of course, wigs can turn a blonde into a redhead, or

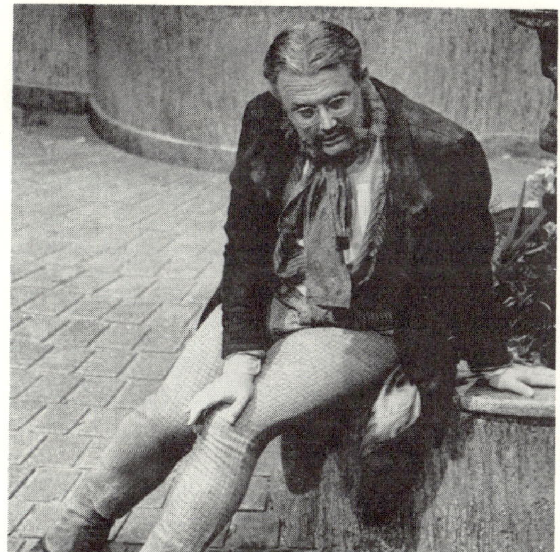

Tight clothing accents portliness. Distressing presents a shabby appearance. Left, Tom Stephenson in *The Miser* (design by Margaret Neuhoff Vida, LPT 1986). Right, dental appliance changes the actor, David Carminito, in *Waking Dreams*. (Dental design by Timothy Peirson, LPT 1985)

make short hair into long, flowing locks.

Special facial and dental appliances made by professional makeup artists can give a young man an old face or a well-groomed man terrible teeth. Contact local professional theaters for resources in your area.

The eye can be fooled with pattern and line. Strong vertical stripes and accented vertical lines will make someone look taller. Bold horizontal stripes will make them look wider. Using shoulder pads and cinching the waist with a corset or a dark contrasting belt will give that waist we mentioned. A skirt hemmed a few inches above the ankles will give a short woman the appearance of more height. A tall woman will look even taller in a shorter skirt because her long legs show. A heavy person will look heavier if their clothes are tight and a small person will look heavier if their clothes are loose.

Modern ankle boots for ladies can be used for nineteenth-century shoes. Men's and women's boots can be modified into eighteenth-century footwear. There is also a

Actors Cynthia Peters, Veronica Smith, and Pamela Turner are converted into barnyard chickens in *The Book of the Dun Cow*.

large selection of replica period-jewelry in department stores these days. It works beautifully on the stage.

How do you make a man into a rooster without putting him in a chicken suit? Select a few characteristics of a rooster—the shock of feathers at his feet, a beautifully feathered breast. Then you translate these characteristics into shreds of glistening fabric, add a fanciful, painted hairstyle, and a rooster you've got.

White satin horns bring us a cow, sparkle poofs on the head of a small woman in pink creates a mouse, and masks and tail feathers galore explode into a coop of cackling hens!

Use your God-given imagination, plan well, be consistent in your design, and you and your audience will be amazed at what costumes can do.

We can't tell you the number of times our costume designer has been at wit's end. Perhaps because of that, she, and we all, have learned to love and rely on another great "production tool"—prayer. We stand amazed at the different ways God has sent help her way—a volunteer calls saying she'd love to sew; the impossible-to-find costume piece seems to fall into her hands; fresh inspiration strikes; or a friend calls with an encouraging word. Remember, He cares about even the tiniest detail, and he cares about you in the midst of all the details!

Costume and hair style allow a woman to portray a man. Veronica Smith is Renfield in *Dracula*. (Design by Kristen Allen, LPT 1987)

9
Sets and Props

All the world's a stage . . .

— William Shakespeare
(As You Like It)

"Could you drop by and tell us what you think of the set for our Christmas pageant? We'd appreciate your ideas!"

Mike Buckley, one of our resident designers, recalls this experience from last December:

A local church called, asking for advice. Now December is one of our busiest production times, but I scheduled a time to stop by their church and see if I could be of any help. As I walked into their gymnasium, I was struck dumb. The set! It was enormous. Spanning the entire width of the cavernous room was a six-foot-high platform on top of which was built an entire Mediterranean town plaza, complete with towers, pillars, and balconies. I approached it, to find the walls wobbly, the stonework crudely painted, and the overall effect pretty shabby. A tired-looking construction supervisor came over. They'd been working for weeks, he told me, and were only two days away from their first performance. He showed me a notebook thick with things still to be done.

I wasn't quite sure what to say, or how I could help. I gave a few suggestions on how to improve the look of the set, but with each suggestion, I saw the weight of his "things to do" list growing in his eyes. They did want my advice for an effect at the climax of the show. It seems that in the script the stone temple was to crumble and then rebuild itself. What?! They didn't need me, they needed Steven Spielberg! I offered a few ideas and wished them the best.

"How sad," I thought as I walked back to my car. How sad that they had locked themselves into movie-style realism. How sad that they underestimated the complexity of building a show of near operatic proportions. How sad that the playwright and the director required impossible special effects when so much could be done simply with inventive scripting and staging.

"Okay, Mr. Design King," a friend of mine challenged, "how would you have done it differently?" Good question, I thought. First, I would have made sure that as set designer I understood the director's concepts early in the process. I could then have suggested more imaginative solutions to the special effects. Second, given the limitation of the work crew and budget, I would not have attempted to recreate a city on stage. An inventive use of abstract pillars, arches, and flats would have been infinitely easier to create and could have worked better to suggest the changes of locale required by the script. Finally, by making the design easier to carry out, the result could be a quality set, painted precisely, and built to be sturdy and safe.

Shaking my head I finished with, "Churches simply have no business doing shows with huge production demands!"

I was proved wrong a week later—at a Christmas program at another friend's church. Once again I was struck dumb by the sight of the set. There in the sanctuary was a New England seacoast village of the 1860s. Snow covered the stage, two-story buildings were cleverly situated, even ships masts appeared in the distance. It was on a grand scale, yet beautifully executed. The colors had been chosen with care, the painting was expertly detailed. During the performance, ice skaters skated on one section of the stage, a scrim-covered storefront revealed tableaus, and it snowed on stage! I had to eat my words.

You see, what it all comes down to is *production value.*

Just What Is Production Value?

Production Value is the overall impact of sets, lighting, props, and costumes. You can have it on a big scale or on a small one. Your show may have small production value of high quality, or big production value that is shabby and cheap. Big is not necessarily better.

Many church drama groups have found it best not to use any set or lighting, and few props or costumes for short sketches. There are several reasons for this choice for small production value. First, the thematic approach of most sketches doesn't require any set. Second, elaborate sets or lighting would not be appropriate for this one small part of the Sunday service. You want your drama to work in concert with all the other elements of the service. And third, with limited resources giving a script big production value is a lot more work.

Whether your presentation's production value is big or small, you want it to be of the best quality. It is quality, not scale that will further the communication to your audience.

Both of the churches we mentioned above wanted big production values. However, they arrived at quite different results. For the first church, it became a monster of discouragement. For the second, it was the glue which held the show together.

What made the difference? *Knowing the resources available, organizing your work,* and *communicating clearly with all involved.*

Resources

When we talk about resources, we're talking about three key areas: *personnel, facilities,* and *budget.*

Personnel. Anyone who has ever put a set together or designed the lighting for a show with big production value knows what an incredible amount of work is involved. For this reason, it's important that you know what kind of help you can count on—what kind of a work crew you can put together. The first church mentioned earlier had designed a set that was too monstrous a project for the personnel available. The results were disappointing for all involved.

If you start with a small project, you'll only need a couple of dedicated people for your first crew. How do you go about recruiting? Begin by asking people you know, putting announcements in your church bulletin, calling local high schools, or making posters. List the skills you need, and make it sound fun!

Start and keep a *crew file.* If your group has a production stage manager, this person would be the one to do this.

Fill out a card for each volunteer noting their name, address, and phone number. List their skills and interests, and when they are or are not available to work. Do they come supplying their own tools or would they be willing to borrow tools for the project?

You will find your crew file to be one of your most valuable assets. Keep it up to date. Add to it as you can. Note each individual's skills based on past performance. For example, Fred proved on the last project that he can't drive a nail to save his life, but look at the great job he did painting that backdrop. What it boils down to is this, don't plan to build the Taj Mahal if the only ones building it will be you and the church custodian!

Facilities. After determining the appropriate production value for a presentation, a designer needs to take into account the limitations of the performance space. Designing a set that is too large for your space makes for a lot of frustration when later it has to be cut down to fit. Be aware of physical obstacles such as awkwardly placed steps, uneven levels, or the visual dominance of a pillar or light fixture. I know one church that has a huge stone pulpit fixed permanently in the center of the platform.

Sometimes the obstacles aren't so much physical as they are traditional. Some churches feel that the presence of a big colorful set is simply inappropriate for the sanctuary, no matter what the function. Look into finding another space for your performance if you can—perhaps the church's fellowship hall or gymnasium. Weather permitting, you may even consider performing outdoors.

If your production is to be an outreach to your community, consider using a local school, small theater, or civic center. This may be an added expense, but the neutral setting will be more approachable for many in your audience, especially those not comfortable entering a church. In any case, determine the limitations of your facility before you begin your design.

Budget. When you first approach the pastoral staff of your church with the idea of starting a drama group, their first concern may be the cost. It's hard enough for churches to find the funds for commitments such as missions and staff salaries. The mention of drama can call up the image of elaborate costumes and sets, and equally elaborate budgets. Reassure them that a drama group can work very well on a modest budget. All that is needed is the actors, the audience, a script, and some imagination.

But there will be times when sets, lights, and costumes are not only appropriate, but necessary. Determine what funds are available and then plan your productions accordingly. Remember, if you are just starting out, start small and budget wisely. Big production value means a larger budget. You may find it possible to increase your budgets by charging admission when and where appropriate. But for now, don't let your designer eyes get bigger than your financial stomach. Do the small things well; then, in time, you may wish to "upgrade" your production value.

Planning Your Design

If this is your first time doing a set design you will more than likely want more information than we can give you here. You can get a lot of help and insight from the books on set design listed in "Further Reading" on page 260. Check in your library for these and other books on stage design and design history. Also, go to see whatever good theater is available in your area, whether it be your local community theater, college productions, or professional companies. You might want to check into the possibility of ushering at a theater to see a performance free of charge. Better yet, ask if they need construction volunteers.

After you have determined the appropriate production value for your presentation and your situation, the work crew you have available, the strengths and weaknesses of your facility, and how much you can afford, you can sit down and start work on your set design.

Whether you're putting together a simple set for a short sketch or a multiple set for a larger production, the steps for your design will be similar.

Concepts. You always start with the script. Even if the script at this point is no more than an idea in someone's head, this is the place to begin.

The script may tell you the time and place of the scene—a living room in the fifties, a hillside in biblical times, a contemporary bus stop. Sometimes the script doesn't set a time or place. As the designer you can dream up your own, or do it without a set altogether. The script may require specific things, in terms of sets or props. A door is slammed, a banana eaten, a lamp turned on. Make notes on all that the script requires.

Next, you will sit down with the director and discuss concepts. He should have some ideas concerning the set. He may even have a detailed picture of exactly what he wants. Or you may be given great license in your design options. The following are questions you'll want to settle with the director:

- What is the theme of the piece?
- What mood do we want to create?
- Is it abstract or realistic?
- Do we want any symbolic pieces?
- How will the actors move in the space?
- What physical elements must we have?

Styles. The most common mistake made by amateur designers (and even some professionals) is assuming that a set must always be realistic.

Part of the blame for this is growing up on a diet of TV and film. In these media, realism is king. If you are watching a courtroom drama on TV, the setting you see looks like a perfectly real courtroom. It doesn't matter that it isn't really a courtroom, but a sound studio dressed up to look like one.

We expect it to look realistic.

But there is no reason to expect realism in theater design. In fact, one of the theater's great strengths is the freedom of it's form. In the theater that courtroom could be represented by a two-dimensional, cartoon-like set; or, an abstract set of oddly shaped, out-of-proportion benches and tables; or, a simple arrangement of folding chairs.

The theatrical set reveals not merely location, but the overall mood of the drama. It impacts the action and engages the audience's imagination. It is this opportunity for engagement that makes theater so potentially powerful. Some of the most memorable productions are those which rely on the active participation of audience imagination. If your set design is always realistic, your drama will lose some of its power to engage your audience.

Fragmentation. So, what are your alternatives to realism? We'll lump them into two categories: The first is *fragmentation* (or "suggested realism").

Let's say your script calls for a suburban kitchen. Pictured in your mind are appliances, table and chairs, walls, windows, doors, cabinets, a dish drainer, plants, and on and on. If you wanted realism, and had the space, labor, and money, you could build a kitchen set just like the one described. Or you could suggest the same realism by fragmentation.

If your set consisted only of a refrigerator, and a kitchen table and chairs, the audience will picture a kitchen. Add a bag of groceries on the table and you suddenly have a *detailed* set. (If it's just a short sketch you could even do without the refrigerator.)

Fragmentation is the limited use of elements in a picture to suggest the complete picture. You can suggest walls or structures by using fragments of architectural details—a window frame floating on its unseen wall (either hung from above or unobtrusively braced from the floor), a free-standing door or empty door frame, an archway hanging overhead, a wall three feet high with a jagged, cutaway top edge to suggest the entire wall. The audience will have no

Notice the use of fragmentation in our set for *Kilts* by David McFadzean. (Design by Mike Buckley, LPT 1988)

trouble seeing the rest of the details with their imagination. Besides, the parts they *imaginatively* build are often an improvement on what can *actually* be built!

Our Lamb's Players production of Robert Bolt's *A Man for All Seasons* called for several locations. The solution: a simple space with varied levels and box-like benches that could be arranged in a variety of ways. For each scene only one element of realism was added to suggest the locale—an actor hung a tree branch and the stage became a garden, a chandelier of candles was lowered and we were transported to the archbishop's chambers, golden banners dropped into sight and we were in Inquisition Hall. Not only did this prevent tiresome scene changes, but it added a rich theatricality to the production.

Abstraction. Another alternative to realism is abstraction. Your script calls for a tree, so you might make the tree out of plastic pipes; paint them blue and attach tin cans

Examples of abstraction: Left, a multi-purpose grid becomes a tree for Chris Causey in *Say No, Max* (Lamb's Players Touring Company 1987) and right, David Heath rides a soft sculpture horse in *Shake the Country* (LPT 1981).

for leaves! By choosing an abstract style for your design, you can highlight special elements, add humor, or clarify the play's theme.

In our production of Eugene Ionesco's *Rhinoceros*, a play about the herd-like conformity in society, we painted all the props and set pieces white. Everything was white—sofas, computer terminals, the hand props, the food, everything except the floor and the costumes. In doing this, the set was helping to illustrate the theme.

While your design must fit the director's concept, help communicate the play to the audience, and be consistent within itself, your choices with abstraction are limited only by your imagination.

For our production of *Damien*, the powerful story of the priest who sacrificed himself to help the lepers of Hawaii, we stacked a mound of platforms and covered it with a large mottled tarp to suggest the island's loneliness. Ragged fishing net hung above suggested the sea, the physical toil, and the decay of leprosy.

Prepare yourself with a thorough understanding of the script and the director's concept, and let your imagination soar.

Set Representations. As your design ideas for the set develop, you'll want to make sketches of them for the director. A sketch will ensure that you are both thinking in the same direction.

If you are working on a show with big production value, you will want to either do a detailed drawing called a rendering, or build a scale model of the set. We tend to build a model when the dynamics of space are important, like an interior setting where the furniture arrangement is crucial to the movement of the actors. The rendering or model is useful not only to the director, but also to the lighting designer, your work crew, and the actors. It lets everybody see the set you have in your mind's eye.

By this point you have established your concept and your style of design, and have made either a sketch, rendering, or model of the set. Before you start the actual construction of the set, you'll want to organize your work.

Set Breakdown. Your first step is to make a *set breakdown.* This is an outlined list of every element that will be a part of your set. It will include such things as:

- Structures such as walls, platforms, and steps
- Floor treatment, such as specialized painting or rugs
- Overhead hanging or *flying* units such as chandeliers or backdrops
- Furniture or other such pieces like tree stumps or refrigerators

The set breakdown should also give an indication of the work involved for each element. Is it to be built, borrowed, rented, bought, or pulled from stock? (*Stock* items are the furniture or other set elements which your drama group already has.)

The following is a sample set breakdown from the Lamb's Players Theatre production of J. B. Priestley's, *An Inspector Calls*.

Set Breakdown:
An Inspector Calls

A. STRUCTURES	
1. Corner platform	build
2. Steps	build
B. FLOOR	
1. Parquet floor peices	stock
2. Tile hearth	build
3. Oriental rug	rent, Old Globe
C. OVERHEAD	
1. Hanging cornices	build
2. Hanging arches	build
3. Hanging window	stock
4. Gazelle head trophy	borrow, Hamilton
5. Chandelier	rent, Old Globe
D. FURNITURE	
1. 2 pedestals w/ busts	buy
2. Victrola cabinet	rent, Grossmont
3. 2 armchairs	rent, Old Globe
4. Fireplace	"
5. Sm. round table	"
6. Settee	"
7. Sofa table	"
8. Credenza	"
9. 2 side chairs	"
10. Lg. round table	stock
11. 2 potted palms	stock pots, buy palms
12. Bench	stock
13. Globe stand	rent, Old Globe

Once the set breakdown has been made, the size of your project will be seen. You may have elements on your list which will need to be built. In the example above they are the platform, steps, hearth, cornices, and arches.

There are two ways that you can approach the construction. The first is to design it as you build it. Grab some wood, a hammer and a saw, and begin. This will work just fine if the project is simple and straightforward. For example, the tile hearth in our set breakdown was a piece of plywood with square tiles attached to it. It was similar to a hearth we had built a few months earlier, so there was no problem using the "design as you build" approach. But often an element is more complicated to construct. In that case it's best to build from *working drawings.*

Working Drawings. Your working drawings can be as simple as a sketch on a scrap of paper noting the dimensions and some indication of how the piece is to be assembled. However, experienced designers usually draw

"Measure twice, cut once"

detailed plans out in scale. Now, you may not be a draftsman, but I encourage you to be as specific with your working drawings as possible.

The more care you take to think through the working drawings, the less chance there is for problems or mistakes in the construction. Also, the clearer your drawings are, the easier it is for someone else to build without having you there. This can free you up to do other tasks, like arranging rental or purchase of all those other things on your set breakdown.

Just as your set renderings will help in your communication with the director, your working drawings will promote clearer understanding with your work crew. Another good planning and communication tool is the *production schedule.*

Production Schedule. This is simply a calendar overview of how you will use the time up to your production's first performance. On the calendar you list each project, who is assigned to it, when it is to be worked on, and the deadline for its completion.

Your production schedule can keep you on track and help avoid those all-night sessions the day or two before your first performance. It will also help you see obstacles ahead of time. You may realize that the steps you need can only be constructed at the performance site. But you can't build there until two days before the opening performance. Seeing that, you schedule Tom to build the cornices first so he can work on the steps later. Or say that Mary, your best painter, is going on vacation during week three of your schedule. So, you schedule the arches to be built the first week so she will have time to paint them during week two.

You will also want to include other items in your schedule. The date that you can put your set into the performance space is called the *load in.* This should be marked on your schedule, along with the dates set for technical and dress rehearsals if you are planning to have them. Also note your plans concerning rentals, purchases, and modifying stock items.

Supervising a Crew. The more elaborate your set design, the more people you'll need to help build it. If you are depending on the hard work of a volunteer crew, a clear schedule and open communication is one of the best ways to show them your appreciation.

If your work crew is large, it is helpful to assign a *crew leader.* This person can help the designer assign tasks, demonstrate construction techniques, and keep the work on schedule.

It may take a little more effort on your part, but make it a point to compliment the work of each individual in your crew. This may seem difficult if their results are not exactly what you had in mind. But remember, the spirit of community and collaboration, of working together on a task, is an important part of what a drama group is all about. Don't let a single-minded focus on the production rob others of their chance to contribute and to grow. If they lack an aptitude for one task, steer them to something different the next time.

Construction. If you find that your group is doing a lot of construction, we suggest you invest in some good quality tools. The right tools, well maintained and stored properly, will last you for years.

It is not the purpose of this chapter to show you how to build a flat or a platform. If you need to construct something and no one in your crew knows how to go about it, there are books that can help. (See the section entitled, *"Further Reading,"* on page 255.) They contain good illustrations with step-by-step instructions. They also include helpful hints about the nuts and bolts of scenery construction.

Again, we also recommend doing volunteer work with a local theater group if you really want to expand your knowledge of stagecraft. Don't be afraid to get professional help if you need it. The small fee for a brief consultation may be well worth the time, energy saved, and the better quality of work.

Set Pieces, Set Dressings, and Props. Now let's look at all those things that were on your set breakdown but didn't need to be built. We divide these items into three categories: *set pieces, set dressing,* and *properties* (or *props*). Think of your set as the bare room of a house you are moving into. Into that room you will put:

- *Set pieces*—all those items you listed under furniture in your set breakdown, including tables, chairs, refrigerators, or tree stumps!

- *Set dressings*—smaller pieces or decorative items which are not used by the actors, such as curtains, table lamps, knickknacks, and books. However, if an actor is to pick up the book and read it, the book is no longer a set dressing but a prop (or *hand prop*).

- *Props*—any item which an actor handles during performance. If you have the personnel, it's a good idea to have one individual responsible for the props and leave the the furniture and set dressing to the set designer. This person is known as the *props master.* Working with the director or stage manager, the props master makes up a list of all the props to be used. On this list, just as on the set breakdown, is noted the task involved to secure each prop. Is it to be made, bought, borrowed,

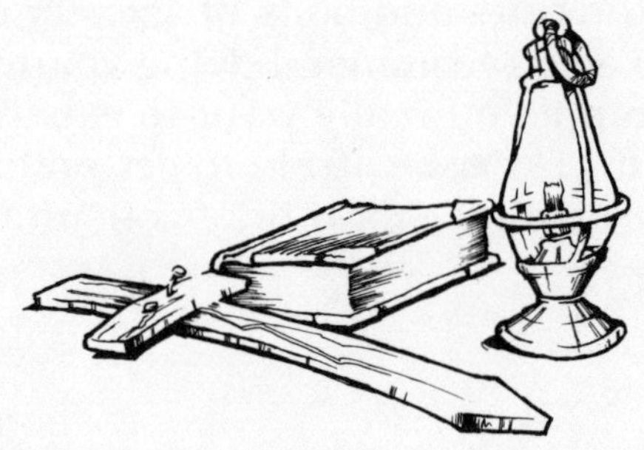

rented, or pulled from stock? Also make a note of any props which need special consideration. Live animals must be cared for. Food props need to be restocked. A letter which is to be torn up needs to be duplicated for each performance.

Obtaining Set Elements

There are five approaches to getting the set elements that you do not build.

Stock. If your drama group is going to be using props with any regularity, it would be worthwhile to develop your own stock. In the long run this can save immeasurable amounts of time and money. Your *stock closet* could be a garage or storage shed or even an unused closet in a Sunday-school room. Make sure you have a place where items can be stored in an orderly manner, so they can be retrieved easily.

You may also want to build some basic set pieces to be part of your stock. A series of nondescript, odd–sized boxes will be handy to use time and again. We know a drama group that uses large, hinged lattice panels as its back drop for all of their Sunday-morning sketches. The simplicity of the panels makes them extremely versatile.

Borrow. We have a friend named Pete who seems to have one of anything you can name—and two of most of them! After our designer has his set breakdown and prop list, and have determined what we have in stock or can build, he gives him a call and ask him about everything else! Borrowing can really stretch your budget. It also keeps you from running all over town to find an item. (Remember Mike, our resident designer? Whenever he is a guest in someone's home, he takes a mental inventory of all their furniture and possessions! That may sound crazy, but it has often come in handy later—when we needed an art deco coffee table he remembered that his friend Pamela has a beautiful one.)

Remember, if you borrow an item you are taking on the serious responsibility to care for it. If a friend is at all reluctant to lend you a priceless heirloom or favorite vase, don't borrow it at all. When you do borrow, make sure the item is returned promptly in good condition. We also send a thank you note and complementary tickets to folks who lend us items. If the worst should happen and the item is lost or damaged, take full responsibility to pay for the item's replacement or repair. That's the very least you can do.

Rent. Renting can be another way to make your dollars do more for you. Many professional theaters and community theaters are happy to rent out their furniture or props. You can often rent things from them which you could never afford to buy. Look at how many pieces on the set breakdown of *An Inspector Calls* were rented from the Old Globe Theatre. The elegant furniture demanded by the show was not in our stock and not in our budget to purchase, but we were able to rent it for a reasonable rate from the larger stock of another theater. The rental policies of theaters and colleges will vary, so by calling around you can often pocket substantial savings.

Another source for rentals can be local antique stores. For 10–15 percent of the purchase price of an item, an antique dealer will often rent it to you. Some items can be found at businesses that handle specialty rentals. Wheelchairs or hospital beds can be rented from medical rental stores. You can find a wide variety of items at party rental stores. If you are planning a contemporary show and need very nice furniture, consider a furniture rental company. Bear in mind that all of these rental companies make their profits from their rentals and so a bargain is harder to come by.

Barter. It takes a pleasantly assertive person to get something for nothing. But you'll be amazed what you can sometimes get with barter. What could you offer a person or business as an incentive in a trade arrangement? Complementary tickets to your production? Free program advertisement? Or a line of special thanks if your program carries no advertisements? I was once able to get $125 worth of carpeting free of charge in exchange for a program ad. (Also, if you are part of a church or a nonprofit organization, remind people that a donation of goods or services can be a tax-deductible contribution.)

Buy. Obviously, buying an item is a lot more expensive than the ideas listed above. But just because you need to buy an item doesn't mean you have to pay a fortune for it. Find the discount stores, thrift stores, and second-hand shops in your area. It takes time and patience, but there are treasures to be found. For our production of *Amadeus* we needed an ornate, Baroque-style chair with a high back. Mike, the set designer, had tried all the usual sources and nearly every antique store in town but could find nothing. He was getting desperate. Then he found an old chair for a real bargain, in a seedy little second-hand store. With some minor upholstery and painting it was absolutely perfect. Visit the thrift stores in your area often and you'll have similar tales to tell.

Create Illusion. It is true that you can't make a silk purse out of a sow's ear, but with a little ingenuity you can make something that *looks* just like one! Develop the sense for seeing the potential in a shabby looking piece of furniture. Can you refinish it, repaint it, or reupholster it? Do you know someone else who could? Part of the challenge and excitement of working with sets and props is to take something seemingly worthless and turn it into something wonderful!

Maybe your drama group is just getting started. Or maybe your group is ready to do more demanding productions. Whatever point you are at in your history, remember that you bear the image of an excellent Creator. Do the very best work that you can!

10
Let There Be Light!

Curtain up, Light the lights
We've got nothing to hit but the heights!

— Stephen Sondheim

Lighting is the one technical element which can give a sketch, staged reading, or play an immediate special something that sets it apart from the ordinary. Bring up the stage lights and a little sketch suddenly becomes theater.

In this chapter we give you an introduction to lighting design and equipment. (If you wish further information, be sure to check the "Further Reading" section located on page 255.) But before we talk about how it all works, you need to ask yourself a few basic questions:

Who Is Your Audience? Lighting is the production element which establishes mood. Because of this, you need to determine for each situation if it is appropriate to use it at all. Let's face it, chase lights, sweeping follow spots, and red computerized concert lighting might not go over too well at your church on a Sunday morning! You might find that extra lighting is best reserved for special events or only for evening

The dramatic mix of light and fog create a storm scene on David Heath and Phil Card in *The Diviners*. (Light design by Dave Thayer, LPT 1986)

services. If all you are doing are short sketches to introduce a sermon, you might not need the benefit of additional lighting at all. If you will be presenting larger productions, or touring to other places, you'll appreciate what good lighting can add.

What Do You Have Now? A church recently asked us to help them improve a poorly lit sanctuary platform. At the time the area was lit by six utility lights like the kind you might use to light a patio. The *lamps* (commonly called "bulbs" outside of the theater) were floodlights designed to light a very wide area. We presented the church with two options: (1) simply replace the floodlights with "spotlight-style" lamps that would focus the light and improve the visibility on the platform, and (2) for even better lighting, replace the current sockets with more sophisticated theatrical instruments of the same wattage. Sometimes a simple upgrade of what you presently have will save you all the problems of a major rewiring to install a new system which might be more than you will ever need.

What Can You Afford? The fact is, lighting is expensive. One theatrical instrument can run $200. A replacement lamp costs another $50 or so. A simple two-scene lighting system with a handful of instruments will rent for more than $150 for a weekend. Later, we'll address borrowing, renting, and acquiring a basic stock as methods of cutting costs, but for now, remember that your budget has to be taken into account before you begin any lighting project.

What Are Your Facilities? There are important space requirements for true theater lighting equipment. Take another look around the front of the facility where you'll be doing your performances. Do you have an impossibly steep-angled ceiling? Do you have a low ceiling? Are there windows which cannot be blacked out with drapes? Would it be possible to have a permanent lighting system installed? Permanent systems can save a great deal of work, but architecturally it might not work for you. Would a portable system work better? Could you hang lighting instruments from the ceiling or walls when you need them, or would it be better to use light trees (free standing poles)?

Which brings us to the issue of wiring. You'll need to determine the power capacities of your building before you start. Recruit some help from your church custodian or someone who knows your building's electrical system. (If you don't know who to ask, find out who the local fire marshall talks to when he comes for an inspection.) Determine exactly how many circuits are in the facility, the capacity of each circuit, if there are any unused circuits available, and if the building's electrical capacity could be increased.

Will You Be Touring? If you will be touring your performances—working in a variety of spaces, from small rooms with no stage, to school cafeterias, to soaring church sanctuaries—then you'll want to look into a portable lighting system. Yes, you could build one of these yourself, with wires, cans, and household dimmers. But don't. The financial savings are not worth the headaches and shabby looks, not to mention the safety risks. There are some excellent small touring systems on the market that are really quite affordable. Educate yourself and don't enter into the situation blindly. Do some research at your library. Take a trip to your local theatrical lighting store and jot down prices.

Equipment

Knowing what kind of lighting instrument to use for a given purpose is something best learned by working with the instruments and observing their qualities at work. However, your local theatrical lighting retailer can give you advice and even demonstrate instruments for you.

Note: If you feel inadequate with all of this, don't despair. Consider bringing in a consultant, as the church with the patio lights did. He can help you determine what your needs are, present some options on how to fill them, and how to stretch your budget. Lighting equipment is a major investment. It is expensive to purchase and maintain. However, there are alternatives to purchasing; here are some suggestions on how to stretch your funds.

Borrowing and Renting. It's usually difficult to borrow lighting equipment because it's expensive, difficult to transport, and most people need to have their equipment always at hand. However, a little persistent legwork could pay off. Try contacting para-church organizations in your area, especially those that have touring performing companies or are involved in youth work. Some of them have equipment they use for concerts or their own drama endeavors and might be willing to let you borrow it. You might also contact area high schools and see how receptive they might be to you borrowing their equipment. You might even suggest a swapping or cooperative arrangement: you borrow some of their equipment this month, they borrow some of yours next month. When push comes to shove, offer to rent their equipment. The worst they can do is say *No.*

Renting from an organization may be an economical solution, but if that is not an option, you might check into renting equipment from your local theatrical lighting supplier. This can be more expensive, but if you rarely use lighting, this could be your best option. Most of these suppliers stock a range of equipment, can help you with free advice, and have a catalogue which they are happy to give you.

Acquiring a Basic Stock. If you plan to use lighting on a fairly regular basis, you will want to develop your own stock of lighting equipment. If you rent a complete system four times a year, then you are throwing away funds which would go a long way toward the purchase of your own system. There is no need to wait until you can afford $10,000 in equipment. You can build up your inventory a little at a time. You might buy a lighting control board this year, a few instruments next year, and more instruments the following year.

Try to find a system that will grow with you. Take time to research what's available. Talk to your local theatrical lighting supplier. Find out what equipment holds up under heavy use. Also keep an eye out for used systems for sale by organizations that are upgrading theirs. It wouldn't hurt to call local churches, schools, theaters, or youth ministries on the chance they might have equipment that they'd like to sell.

The Versatile Followspot. A followspot is a movable instrument that throws a focused beam of light. Though it looks too theatrical for applications where natural looking light is wanted, it can often save money by doing the work of several instruments. The youth choir at the church one of our designers attends was doing a musical production about Joseph. They asked him if he would provide the lighting. The budget restricted him to renting a very small system from a lighting supply company. The number of instruments was inadequate for lighting the length of the huge platform, so he decided to use the instruments to create two different-colored washes onstage. (This process is described in greater detail later in this chapter.) The washes could effectively change the moods of various scenes and songs while the lighting for soloists and the narrator would be provided by a single followspot operated from the balcony.

A followspot has multiple gel frames built in, so the operator is able to change colors for mood variations. Another plus is that a followspot can be operated independently of a lighting control board. Just remember that a followspot's light is not realistic and tends to flatten out a performer if used only by itself. But in the right situation it can be a workable budget-stretcher.

The Basics of Lighting Design

Let's start by repeating ourselves. The best way to begin as a novice designer is to get out and see as much good theater as possible. This is even more important for the

General lighting focuses the action on stage. Ken Wagner, Steve Multer, and Mike Gier in *Cotton Patch Gospel*. (Light design by Brett Kelly, LPT 1988)

lighting designer. Photos in books are rarely able to show the subtleties that are possible with lighting.

Lighting is an intuitive design form which is difficult to describe verbally. However, there are some basic principles which can be learned. These are the principles we want to cover here. But remember—getting out, seeing it, and then doing it yourself is the best way to learn. Arm yourself with this basic knowledge, then go look at a play and critique its lighting. Can you see all the action clearly? Is the light design living up to the responsibilities listed below?

Six Functions of Lighting

Visibility. The first and most obvious function of lighting is visibility. Odd as it may seem, the most difficult lighting effect to achieve is a smooth, even illumination of the stage. But good lighting involves more than just seeing the performers onstage. Remember the church with the patio lights? With their floodlights on, you could see the pastor, but from the back pew you couldn't tell whether he had his eyes opened or closed. The dim, spotty lighting prevented him from carrying his facial expressions beyond the front rows. (Some pastors may not like to hear this, but if we can't see you, we can't really hear you, and if we can't hear you, we may fall asleep!)

Mood. The second function of lighting is the creation of mood. A play or sketch's thematic content can often be emphasized by good lighting, whether the piece is a somber drama, a farcical comedy, or a sparkling musical. It's the

Single source lighting creates a dramatic mood. Carolyn Schade in *The Miracle Worker.* (Light design by Dave Thayer, LPT 1983)

lighting designer's job to take the theme of the script and the director's interpretation of the mood and translate them into light. Once again, here's where realism is often harder to achieve than a stylized interpretation, and usually not as fun.

Focus. The third function of lighting is to direct the audience's focus. In movies, the camera zooms in or cuts to another point of view. It determines where the audience is looking. On the stage, the lighting designer helps to direct that focus. For example, when an important character makes her entrance at the top of the stairs, you can make her the center of attention by subtly bringing down the level of the other stage lights while bringing the level of light up on her.

Time. What time of day is it onstage? Is it dawn, morning, high noon, late afternoon, sunset, early evening, midnight? Each of these times has a distinct look, both indoors and out, and the lighting designer can give us this information.

Locale. Where does the action of the sketch or play take place? Are we at an outdoor picnic, a smokey nightclub, or a dim funeral parlor? Obviously, the set carries much of the responsibility for suggesting the locale, but the lighting can lend extra support.

Climate. This is subtle, but the fact that noon in the Sahara looks different than noon in Siberia can help our imaginations feel the temperature of a given place.

Qualities of Light

Let's explore, for a moment, what we call the four *qualities of light.* These are the tools a designer uses to establish these six *functions* of light we've just discussed.

Brightness. The first quality is the obvious element of brightness (or intensity). This figures predominantly in establishing *visibility*, of course, but it's also important for creating *mood* and *time*. Try turning on one table lamp in your living room this evening. What can you see clearly? What is the mood created? Is any one thing in focus? Then turn on every light in the room. How do these things change?

Angle. Light travels in straight rays emanating from its source. The angle at which a light hits an object helps set time, climate, and mood. Try an experiment with a flashlight in front of a mirror some night. Turn off all other lights. Hold the flashlight over your head and shine its light on your

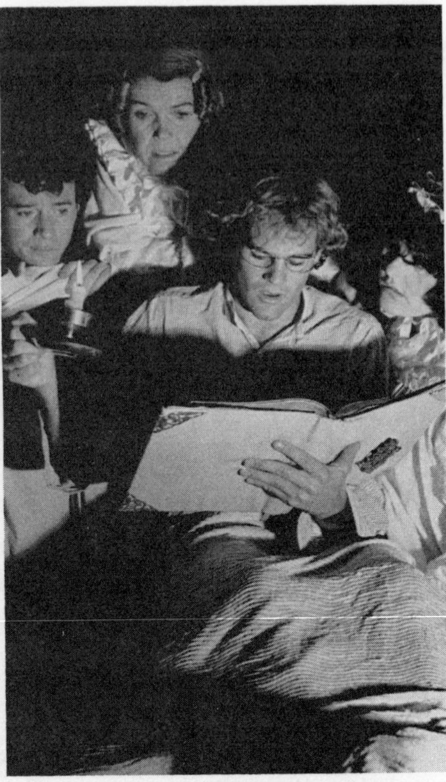

The angle and intensity of lights help to set different moods. Left, Dave Heath, Deborah Gilmour Smyth, and Rick Meads in our adaptation of *Dracula*. (Light design by Mike Buckley, LPT 1987) Right, Robert Duckett, Veronica Smith, Mark Coterill, and Pamela Smith read a bedtime story in *Once Upon a Star*. (Light design by Dave Thayer, LPTC 1986)

face. What effect does that angle have on lighting your face? Now try shining it up from below your chin. How has the effect changed? Try all different angles from the side, from behind, from straight-on, and observe the difference each angle makes.

Color. The third quality of light is color. Placing a piece of *gel* (colored transparent plastic) in the beam of a light changes the color and feel of that light. You'll need some colored gels to experiment with this using your flashlight. (A swatch book of gels is available at your local theatrical lighting supply store for a small charge.) Try different colors projected on your face. How does your face look with a pale pink light? How is it different under green light? Color does a lot to establish mood, time, and locale.

Distribution. The last quality of light is called distribution. This is how a beam of light is distributed on an object. Is it concentrated and focused, or diffused and softer? To better understand this quality, get your flashlight again. Shine it on your face from the side. Notice the clearly defined shadows and the intensity of the light on your cheek. Now hold a piece of gauze or thin white paper over the flashlight. This light will be more diffused and soft. How have the shadows and intensity of the light changed? Distribution helps set mood, focus, and climate.

Think through these four qualities of light in conjunction with the six functions of stage lighting. How could you combine different qualities of light to establish mood, locale, and climate? For example, what effect would be created by a bright light, angled from below, with a red color, and in tight focus?

Carrying It Off

The following steps are a general overview of how to carry out a lighting design. We'll be approaching the design as if it were for a longer dramatic work with specific lighting needs. A short sketch, or a production which needs only general illumination, can adapt these principles to fit. Remember though, that there is no substitute for hands on experience. This can often be gained from class work at a local college or volunteer work at a local theater.

The first step in approaching a project is the same for any designer—read the script. Make note of themes, moods, and logistical requirements, like time of day, locale, and climate. Then sit down with the director and discuss his concepts for the production. List all the ways that lighting can help the production. Make sure you understand the layout of the set. From here, you're ready to transfer your ideas into arrangements of light.

Drafting a Lighting Plot

Varying types of lighting help you accomplish different objectives. For example:

- *Area lights,* which give general illumination to areas of the stage
- *Washes,* which provide floods of specific color to alter mood
- *Specials,* which are used for specific focus, such as illuminating one actor or object
- *Toning lights,* which are used to illuminate and texture portions of the set

Let's say our production needs good, thorough area lighting, washes of amber and blue, a special on the stairs for a musical number, a blue gel special shining in through a window for a night scene, and a toning light on a set piece which hangs overhead. Just as with a set design, the lighting should first be thought out on paper. Make a list of all the lighting equipment you have available. Now you're ready to start laying out your arrangement, marking off instruments as you put them into your light plot.

The lighting plot is best done by drafting to scale an overhead view of the set. Draw in any permanent lighting equipment. Then draw where you plan to hang other lights, such as on overhead pipes, and light trees. Using a template of lighting instruments (available at your lighting supplier), draw in each instrument you plan to use in its hanging position. Consider angles of light and the location of set pieces.

Careful planning ahead of time will insure you have enough instruments for all your needs (or else let you know how many instruments you'll need to secure from other sources). Make any needed corrections on your plot before you proceed to hang the actual instruments.

Hanging. With your light plot handy, you are now ready to hang the instruments in their positions. This may mean first creating the positions to hang them from. If you need to, put up pipes or set up light trees. When you hang the instruments, it's not necessary to circuit (electrically connect) them, or to focus them in the same step (although it's certainly possible). It is less confusing to do it one step at a time and it allows you to divide the steps of lighting into more manageable tasks. For example, you might hang the lights tonight, circuit them tomorrow, and focus them on Saturday.

Hanging instruments is physically demanding labor and it always goes faster if you have a crew to help you. If you have a crew of untrained volunteers, begin with a brief lesson on the basics. If you yourself are unsure of how to hang the instruments, hands-on experience is the only teaching method. Make sure that any instrument is securely fastened at its position. If it hangs directly over the audience or the stage, make sure it also has a *safety chain* attached to both the instrument and the pipe.

Circuiting. Circuiting the instruments is simply the process of supplying each instrument with electrical power. It helps to think of electricity as *juice.* For example, if two instruments are circuited (plugged) into one cable and you turn on the juice in that cable, then both instruments will come on. All your instruments need to be connected to whatever control board you are going to use. You may be using a computerized board, a manual two-scene board or a homemade rheostat board. Or, you may even be using an existing or improved system in your sanctuary, but all your instruments need to be controlled from one place. Your control board will have a certain number (be it four or forty-eight) of dimmers or channels which it can control. Each dimmer has a certain amount of electrical power which it can distribute to a given number of circuits, and the circuits to a given number of instruments. If you turn on the juice in one dimmer, all the lights circuited into that dimmer will come on.

If you are going to install a permanent lighting system in your facility, you'll be able to run cables to certain lighting positions and leave them in place. You may even be able to run them through the building's structure itself and keep a tangle of cabling out of sight. This would be the optimum situation, of course, but you may not be so fortunate. You may need to set up a portable lighting system and lay yards of cable every time you circuit your lights. If this is the case, you'll want to allow for this extra time when scheduling your crew.

Note: Make sure you know the maximum wattage each dimmer can handle. Add up the total wattage of lamps you plan to circuit into each dimmer. If that amount is more than the dimmer's maximum capacity, rethink your circuiting.

Focusing the Lights. Now that you have the instruments hung and circuited, you are ready to focus. A light is focused by pointing it at the exact place you want to illuminate. This procedure works best with at least two people, one to handle the instrument and one to act as the object or area to be lit. It's important to focus in relative darkness. (You'll want to take this into consideration if your facility cannot be darkened during the day.) First, place a dot of tape on the floor of the stage corresponding to the center of each area that appears on your plot. Determine each instrument's function as noted on the plot. Let's say that the first instrument we're going to use is one to focus on area *A*.

The person onstage stands on the dot of tape which corresponds to area *A*, and the person focusing the light adjusts it to shine on the face of the person onstage. (It is important that a light be focused on the head of the person onstage and not focused on the dot of tape on the floor. Your purpose is to light the performer's face, after all, and not his feet.) Once the instrument is focused correctly, secure it in place and move on to the next instrument.

Instruments should be focused one at a time to avoid the confusion of having two lights on at the same time. It is possible to have more than one person focusing—one person readying his instrument while the other's is on. I find that focusing goes most efficiently when two or three people are focusing in turn.

Setting the Cues and Levels. The lighting designer and the director then meet for what is called the *paper tech*. Here the *light cues* for the production are determined. Cues are the places in the production where there is a change in lighting. A cue could be the lights coming up at the beginning of a scene, the sudden flash of lightning outside a window, or the slow setting of the sun as a scene progresses. The cues are agreed upon and noted by the stage manager who will refer to them during the performance. Each cue is assigned a number. The timing for each cue is also established. For example, the lightning flash is very quick, but the sunset has a long time assigned to it.

With input from the director, the designer then decides on the desired look for each cue. This is called *setting levels.* He might want the first scene to look cheerful and the second scene to look somber. He experiments by setting the dimmers at various levels of brightness until the desired look is achieved. The level of each dimmer is recorded for each numbered cue. The light board operator will set the dimmers at the level decided upon by the designer. To "take cue number seven," should translate into giving the audience exactly the look that the designer and director specified for that cue.

Technical and Dress Rehearsals. Once the cues and levels are set, you are ready for a *technical rehearsal,* or *tech.* This rehearsal is designed to introduce the technical elements of the production into the show that the actors have been rehearsing. (This step may not be necessary if the show isn't technically demanding.) The technical rehearsal is for the benefit of the lighting designer, the stage manager, and the operator of the lighting control board (which may be one and the same person). Patience is required by all involved. Technical difficulties often need to be ironed out by stopping and repeating cues again and again.

The first step of a technical rehearsal is called a *cue-to-cue.* In a cue-to-cue, only those parts of the show where lighting cues occur are rehearsed. For example, lights coming up at the beginning of the scene is rehearsed with the actors making their entrances and speaking their first few lines. They are then stopped and instructed to pick up with their lines just prior to the next cue. If there are no cues until the end of the scene, then they are instructed to begin from there. Each cue is repeated until all are satisfied that the lighting is correct. It's customary to rehearse any recorded sound cues in this manner at the same rehearsal.

Once all the cues have been rehearsed in this way, it's time to try a run-through of the entire show, inserting all the sound and light cues at their proper times. This run-through helps the actors see how the technical elements work into their performances. More importantly, it solidifies the cues for the lighting and sound operators. It may be necessary to stop from time-to-time during this run-through to further refine the execution of the cues and even repeat cues that are causing problems.

After the technical rehearsal, we start *dress rehearsals*, where other elements such as costumes and props are added to the show. The objective of a dress rehearsal is to simultaneously create a "performance-quality" run-through and iron out any last-minute bugs. Although a dress rehearsal might have to be stopped to overcome a major problem, the goal is to achieve performance quality as soon as possible. During dress rehearsals all the designers take notes of things which need to be corrected. The lighting designer watches to make sure that there are no unevenly-lit spots on the stage and that all the pictures he has created with light are satisfying the needs of the production.

Lighting is a great way to accentuate the vitality of drama. It can strengthen a mood, and it can intensify communication. From books you can learn the basics, but you will not learn everything you need to know from books. It is with observation and hands-on experimentation that you become really knowledgeable. The limitations of your facility and budget may test your creativity and resourcefulness, but give it a shot. Done well, your lighting can be dazzling!

11
Getting the Word Out

It's a war in the marketplace. Today's marketing manager must—and can—plan like Alexander the Great, maneuver like Napoleon, and fight like Patton.

—Al Ries and Jack Trout
(Marketing Warfare)

Now hold on a minute!" you say. "Who's at war? We're just a little drama group, see? It's not like we're competing with Avis and Hertz! Besides, who's got a marketing manager?!"

True, yours may only be a small church drama group. And, you may be the person who has been put in charge of the posters. Or, you alone may be the director, the stage manager, the technical staff, *and* in charge of publicity! Or, maybe you're part of a larger group hoping to develop a larger audience. Whatever your situation, you can make your job go more smoothly by learning some of the principles of marketing.

"Whoa! We're not selling cereal, deodorant, or automobiles here! We're not out to make a buck! We're a group of Christians working with drama to communicate some important things to our audience."

Exactly! And you want your communication to be

effective, don't you? You want your audience to know about you and to attend your performances, right? All right then. You can learn some tips from the experts. Call it marketing or call it publicity, it means getting the word out on what you have to offer.

Remember the advice of Jesus, "Be wise as a serpent, yet gentle as a dove." Be wise! Be resourceful. Understand what the situation needs. Look beyond the surface, . . . but don't manipulate. Let love be your aim.

Jesus gave this advice to his disciples about to embark on their own "touring production." It is the difference between a calculated seduction of your senses by a perfume ad campaign and the honest desire to serve the public by informing them about your work. We are serving our audience. We can be assertive in our marketing campaigns without feeling dishonest. Profit is not our aim—service is. Our goal is to leave our audience enriched, challenged, and, hopefully, one step closer to wholeness.

This chapter is a crash course on the fundamentals of marketing, with an emphasis on publicity. You don't need thousands of dollars to have a distinctive knock-out publicity plan. All it takes is a little hard work and some wisdom gleaned from the professionals. Whether you're selling lemonade on the street corner, fast food around the world, or theater to your community, the basics of marketing are the same.

Corporations spend millions of dollars each year to determine whether or not they are "hitting the mark" with their publicity. The following questions help them evaluate and re-evaluate their success. Answer them and you will be on your way to finding a marketing plan custom-fit to your group.

1. *What do you want to accomplish?* This is a vital question for any group starting out. It should be answered by your *mission statement* (discussed in the chapter 2). Everyone in your group should be able to answer this question clearly and succinctly.

2. *What is the value of your service to the audience?* What's so important about your work? Why should they come see you or have your group come and perform for them? Determine the benefits to your audience. "What will I get out of this?" is the first question people ask before responding to publicity.

Thus, theater ads cry out—*LAUGH, THRILL, CRY—SPARKLING, INTRIGUING*—or—*EASY TICKET EXCHANGE, NO LINES, 40 PERCENT OFF, GET ONE SHOW FREE!!* All of these words appeal to some basic need or desire in human nature.

During the Civil War, Abraham Lincoln was often seen at the opera or theater. When criticized for such "trivial pursuits" during wartime, he replied, ". . . it rests me. I love to be alone and yet with other people. I want to get this burden off. . . . A hearty laugh relieves me, and I seem better able to bear my cross."

The benefit you offer may not only be diversion or a lightening of the load, it may also be education, or inspiration. But remember, outside of your family and friends, people won't come to your performances because they *should* but because they *want* to. For this reason, your publicity materials must make your production sound and look appealing. The audience must see some kind of potential benefit. Bob Ainsworth of the United Way put it best—"It's not what *you* have to sell—it's what *they* want to buy!"

3. *Who is your audience?* In chapter 2 we discussed the importance of this question. You have to identify your audience before you know how to appeal to them. By aiming your production and publicity at that specific group, you will get a higher response. Consider geographical location, age, occupation, income and education levels, ethnic background, and special interests. You don't have to hire an outside marketing research firm—do some questioning of your own. All it takes is time. Draw up a survey questionnaire asking for this information and hand it out. The answers you get back will tell you a lot about the people you're trying to reach.

4. *What kind of image do you want to present?* What do you want your publicity materials to say about you? Will they be elegant or earthy? Will they say you are professional or amateur? Serious or comic? Conservative or radical? Do they show stability or do they cry for help? Do you want to proclaim that you are Christians or do you want people to gradually discover that? It is important that the expectations that your audience holds from your publicity materials be very close to what they actually get. This is where a good graphic designer can offer help. (More on this later in the chapter.)

5. *What is your competition?* You say you don't have any? Ah, but you do. There may be no other drama group in your church, but you have competition all the same. Television, movies, sports, concerts, school functions—all of these vie for time and attention. Why should someone opt for your show rather than some other attraction? When you have that answer formulated, publicize this uniqueness—loud and clear.

You may not be competing with the professional theater in your town, but don't miss out on the opportunity to study their marketing techniques. While it is important to maintain your own unique image, you can learn a lot from other's mistakes and successes. Set up an appointment with their marketing directors. They would most likely be happy to offer some advice.

Finally, be aware of conflicting schedules. The night of the mother-daughter banquet or the seventh game of the World Series may not be the best time to schedule your largest theater production of the year!

The Marketing Plan

A successful marketing plan includes three elements:

- Use of the media
- Promotional materials
- Personal communication

And each of these elements must accomplish three things:

- Inform
- Generate interest
- Solicit response

The Media. Whether it is your church bulletin or your local paper, a small radio station or network TV, the media can provide you with *free* publicity. While a notice in the bulletin may only involve a call to the church secretary, the way to communicate to your newspaper is with the press release. (For a sample press release, see Appendix D on page 253.) Newspaper editors require vast amounts of news to fill their pages and they depend heavily on press releases to keep them informed. However, there is a lot of competition for space and stacks of press releases arrive at their paper every day. To get yours read and printed here are some important rules:

- Begin with a punchy headline. Think of some unique and interesting angle to grab the attention of the reader. Remember your competition.

- In the first two paragraphs tell Who, What, When, Where, Why, and How.

- Keep the sentences short and to the point. Be specific. Avoid jargon, slang, and words that are difficult to understand.

- Be factual. Give important names, dates and information. Include items of interest such as awards or recent accomplishments.

- Do not blow your own horn. Stay away from superfluous adjectives like *greatest*, *best ever*, and *most amazing.* You are not writing ad copy!

- The story should be double-spaced and typed on one side of the paper. If you have more than one page, type the word *more* at the bottom. On consecutive pages repeat the headline and add page numbers. Centered at the end of the release type the word *End* or ###.

- Put the name of your group and a contact person with phone number at the top right of each page.

- Put the date at the top.

- Make sure you know the deadlines for all the publications you will be mailing to. Make sure the name of the paper's contact person is up-to-date and spelled correctly.

Feature Articles. Your local newspapers carry feature articles dealing with human interest stories and profiles. Very often there is a separate editor for these sections. Write a letter to this person telling her your proposal for a story about your group or production and why you think it would make a good article for her section or column. Give a phone number where the editor or columnist can get in touch with you if she wants to pursue it. Along with your letter include an *organizational fact sheet.*

Organizational Fact Sheet. Often, interested reporters or other parties want to know more about the organization. This piece should answer questions like: *Who's in charge? How did you get started? What else have you done? How are you funded? Are you full-time? What are the creden-*

tials of staff members? This is the perfect way to get information out that might otherwise be overlooked. You'll want to update this periodically.

Public Service Announcements. (See Appendix D on page 254 for an example.) Radio and television are powerful tools for mass communication; and it just so happens that they are required by law to broadcast free public service announcements for nonprofit organizations. That can mean free advertisement for your group over the airwaves! Since your listing is usually limited to about fifteen seconds, you will need to keep the information in your press release to a tight, informative paragraph. Your public service announcement (PSA) should be read aloud and timed to make sure it is the correct length. Some television stations will even show color slides or a short video when they run the PSA. Check with your local PSA directors from each station for more information.

Promotional Materials Promotion materials are another way to get the word out. They can grab attention, give information, and ask for a response. With wise planning you can produce quality materials for little cost. Most of your promotional materials will be in two areas: (1) *posters* and *flyers*, and (2) *direct mail.*

1. *Posters and flyers:* A sharp, well-designed poster can be an inexpensive way to promote a perform ance. Most of the space on the poster should be given to graphic elements like a strong photo or illustration. These need to non-verbally call out, "Stop! Wait! Over here. You don't want to miss this!" Once you have their attention people should be able to find all the necessary information easily. Titles, names, location, dates, times, cost, and phone numbers must be included along with a brief synopsis of the play or other intriguing copy. Be selective with how you use posters, however. They

are not effective in all situations. You will find they work best in churches, schools, bookstores, and some coffee shops. They are not very effective in stores, on telephone poles, or around your community at random. Flyers should be designed like small posters. They can be handed out, inserted in bulletins, sent through the mail, or tacked up like posters. Many of the fundamentals of graphic design discussed below will also apply to posters and flyers.

2. *Direct Mail.* Some small groups will have no real need to use direct mail. Posters around the church or flyers inserted in the bulletin will be enough to do the job. But if you want to draw the surrounding community to your performance space, or are trying to book a touring production,

then it is important that you understand direct mail. Direct mail is the sending of flyers, newsletters, brochures, or marketing letters to a select list of people. Your first task with direct mail is rather obvious. You need a list of people to mail to! Develop a mailing list for your group. Start with your church membership list, ask local church associations for their directories, ask your group members and friends to give you copies of their Christmas card lists, get copies of local Chamber of Commerce directories, rent lists from other groups. Have name and address slips inserted in all your programs or sign-up sheets at all your performances. If you have the budget you can rent the mailing lists of other groups or use a professional mailing list service.

Direct mail really is a battleground. Tons of ads, brochures, newsletters and flyers fill our mail boxes daily. The competition for attention is intense. How can you stand out?! What will make them stop to read yours before they file it with the rest of the junk mail?

The answer lies in the proper use of two skills: *Writing Copy* and *Graphic Design.*

Writing Copy

You can't just sit down and dash off a great piece of direct mail copy. It is hard work. There are no shortcuts. Almost without exception, the success of any direct mail piece is in direct ratio to the time spent on its preparation. Work at it until you've got the best piece possible.

Let's look at some sure-fire, tried-and-true principles. These fundamentals work, whether you're promoting lemonade or theater.

Pull 'em In! The purpose of any element in a poster, brochure, ad, or letter is to get your audience to read the first sentence! You have just seconds to grab the reader's interest. The first thing they see must draw them in. It may be a dramatic statement showing a benefit—"You'll never laugh so hard in your life!" or an intriguing statement—"Baked Lasagna Enclosed!" or a provoking question—"When was the last time you kicked your dog?" Whatever it is, it is worth the time spent to get it right. Don't stop with a few suggestions—write, write, write! Remember—your headline must lead them to the first sentence. You don't want a headline that makes the reader waste time in trying to figure it out.

Keep It Simple. Samuel Johnson was quoted as saying, "He is a benefactor of mankind who contracts the great rules of life in short sentences that may easily be impressed on the memory, and so recur habitually to the mind."

Dr. Johnson understood one of the first laws of writing copy—clarity and brevity breed remembrance. If you want to be understood, and if you want your words and ideas remembered, keep your copy clear and brief.

Admit it! Do you read all the newsletters, brochures, and flyers that come your way? Of course not. And most people don't have the time, or want to take the time, to read your material either, so make it easy for them. All your words, sentences and paragraphs should be short. Just like in poetry, the selection of each word is important. You must hold the reader's attention. They should be able to get any important information within seconds. Brevity and focus will help them to remember—and to respond.

Repeat, Repeat, Repeat. Be redundant. Repeat yourself. Tell your story over and over in different ways. Studies show that people forget 65 percent of what they have learned an hour after learning it—and 80 percent of it within twenty-four hours! You can see the importance of simple, clear communication.

No Wading Allowed. There should be no confusion. All your copy needs to act like a funnel moving your reader to the response. After you have their attention, it's important that you lead them through with a logical progression. Sometimes numbering the elements or underlining important points can help. Try breaking up the copy with subheads and dashes.

Who Says. Quotes or testimonials can boost your credibility. Often, if you're just starting out, you can solicit a quote by calling someone well-known in the community who might be sympathetic to your organization. Ask around. You'd be surprised at the number of people that would be open to lending you a hand in your publicity. Don't be afraid to tell them the kind of quote you are looking for! If they do respond, be accurate. Don't misquote or manipulate a quote out of context. Honesty maintains your credibility—it is good publicity itself!

Ask for a Response. Don't just inform, ask for a response. What do you want the readers to *do*? What action do you want them to take? Ask them to take it! Whenever you end an ad, a brochure, or a letter, ask the readers to respond. Then help them to respond by enclosing a return postcard, a response envelope, or having a phone number printed in large type. On the response device use words like: *Yes! I'm interested in booking this powerful production. Please contact me!* or *Order now! Limited seats available!!* or *Don't miss out! Call today!* Urgency will help them to respond right away rather than to put it off and forget about it.

Work as a Team. If you will be writing the copy, work closely with the graphic designer. It's important that you both have input from the beginning. A designer will know how to attract the reader's attention graphically and lead the reader's eye through the piece. Even if you don't have, or can't afford, a designer, you can learn the principles of good graphic design. A little study goes a long way. Remember, the copy and the graphic design are working together to lead the reader to a positive response.

Graphic Design

We all respond to good composition and design whether we are aware of it or not. One of the hallmarks of our culture is the great amount of quality graphic design all around us. According to Theater Marketing Director, Craig Palmer:

> Most people form their impressions of performing arts groups from secondary sources—comments of friends, posters, advertising pieces and the like—not from actual performances. A good design system serves to motivate and reinforce these impressions.

But using design well is no easy task. The road to effective design is strewn with those who traveled only by their instincts rather than by learning a few basic principles.

Even if you don't have the budget to work with a designer, take the time to learn these basics. The general public may not understand why something is pleasing to the eye, but you can. Study what good designers produce and you will able to avoid many of the common mistakes.

The Logo. The first design element your drama group or organization will want is a logo. This is your graphic signature. Your logo should be clean and simple and yet describe your group. It can let us know something of your purpose. It will give us a different flavor if its style is playful, classic, or modern. Here are two examples of logos used by Lamb's Players:

The company's name is clear and distinctive. The use of the word *Lamb* gives a hint to the company's Christian perspective. Notice the abstract of the lamb's head in the shield. The shield design alludes both to the comedy/tragedy masks and the shields and crests used by the medieval traveling troupes that presented the early morality plays.

Once you have settled on a logo, you should use it on all your printed material. People will come to identify it with you and you with it. While nothing is ever absolute in design, here are some principles that will help make yours strong and clear:

Communicate. Good design is good communication! You hear that? Memorize it! You may be able to draw a pretty picture or produce wonderfully ornate calligraphy, but pretty or artsy doesn't sell! In fact, it may even get in the way—making it more difficult for someone to understand and respond to your message.

Good graphic design has type, photographs, illustrations, and color working together to communicate one clear unified message. The design is subordinate to the message. When design is done solely for the sake of design, communication is diminished. So, first decide what to say, and *then* decide how to display it.

Less Is Best. Most beginners clutter their design with too many elements. This makes it hard to understand. The reader isn't sure where to start, gives up, and drops that beautiful piece in the trash with the rest of the junk mail! The answer? Simplify.

Center of Visual Interest. Establish this by using a minimum of focal points. Usually you will use only one, or at most two, elements of interest. This is the first thing that

catches the eye. It might be a headline, a photo or a graphic illustration. All other elements will be smaller and less focused, and even these other elements should be limited in number.

Line It Up. Too many elements slanted different directions causes confusion. Use a minimum amount of axes of alignment. This way you can lead the reader's eye around the page in the sequence you desire.

Unity. When all the parts are related, the reader has no question about the message. Accomplish this by making sure all your design elements are consistent. One technique is to repeat a specific theme, word, or graphic throughout the piece. Another is to use a minimum amount of typefaces. Most experts agree that you should not use more than two in any one piece. Unity makes for quick and easy viewing.

Balance. This is another element in making your design pleasing to the eye. It enables the viewer to absorb all the information rather than only one part. No one part should outweigh another. Since readers are drawn to the large or dark elements, don't put them all on one side—instead balance them on the page. This will help keep the eyes moving throughout the piece. While balance is important, you don't want everything symmetrical. This can make your design bland or stilted. Work for asymmetrical balance.

Balance one large element with two smaller ones. Don't match elements size for size.

Contrast. This is where your publicity comes alive! You can set the eye in motion by breaking a piece up with contrasting elements. But be careful here—too many contrasting elements create clutter, while just the right amount leads the eye in a logical rhythm to the heart of your piece. Some examples of contrast:

- Using a sans serif headline with a serif body text
- Breaking up a long paragraph with subheads
- Using call-out or stand alone quotes
- Using bullets and boxes

If you use a three-column format in a newsletter, try breaking it up with a two-column graphic or photo. The three-column format on an 8 1/2- by-11-inch newsletter is more interesting and gives you more opportunities for adding variety than the one- or two-column format.

Try using *ragged right* formatting on your columns—the uneven lines add a subtle contrast that is often more appealing than a symmetrically justified column. A square element will be a strong contrast on a page dominated by horizontal and vertical rectangles.

The Golden Rectangle. The Greeks thought that the most aesthetically appealing shape was a rectangle with sides in a three-by-five ratio. They built their classic temples and buildings based on this ratio. Today we continue to follow in their footsteps. Placed in a vertical position, this *golden rectangle* creates the strongest graphic image. Even taken to an extreme two-by-five ratio, the rectangle is a powerful design element, whether used vertically or horizontally.

White Space. Don't be afraid of the *negative space* (blank space) on your page. Used properly, it can call attention or bring pleasing relief to the eye. Keep your white space pushed out to the margins. Don't trap it inside your layout, but be careful—too much white space around each element creates a floating effect. Keep the elements in groups with the white space outside.

The Thumbnail Sketch. A thumbnail sketch is a fast and effective way to work out your design before you get to the final layout. Decide on what your elements are—text, headline, illustration, photo—and sketch them on a sheet of paper. You will quickly be able to tell if it's balanced, has unity, contrast, repetition, rhythm, and proper white space. This step is an invaluable, time-saving tool. Once the design is agreed upon, it's simply a matter of putting in all the pieces.

Typography

There are few ironclad rules about the use of type, but here are a few tips to keep in mind:

1. In headlines, unless there are three words or less, use upper and lower case. Studies have shown that all caps are hard to read.

2. When headlines accompany body text, keep them close together.

3. Printers measure type size in *points*. Never use type smaller than nine-point in body text.

4. Don't mix two serif typefaces in one piece. Instead use a different point size or weight within the same family of type. This gives a variety while keeping consistency.

5. *Do* mix a serif typeface with a sans serif type (i.e., a sans serif headline with a serif body text).

6. Don't reverse out copy. White type on a black background is harder to read. The exception would be a heading or small amount of copy.

7. Use italics sparingly. It is also harder to read in large quantities. Some italics are harder to read than others. A sans serif italic can create energy, especially in a headline.

8. Break your headlines in logical places.

9. And, finally, as mentioned before, take the time to learn from what the professionals are doing. Start a file of design pieces you like. Copy, borrow, and use the best ideas. Keep in mind that you don't have to re-invent the wheel!

Photography

A picture really can be worth a thousand words, especially in theater publicity. Crisp, dynamic photos can be one of your strongest tools. They are valuable additions to posters, marketing brochures, and newsletters. They can also help bring you to the attention of the media and potential sponsors.

The performing arts present the perfect source for good photographs. See if someone in your drama group or in your church has experience in photography. If your budget can afford it, you might want to schedule a session with a professional. But don't look for your photographer at the nearest portrait studio. If you can't find a theater photographer, look for a photojournalist or sports photographer. They are more accustomed to working with live action.

Good publicity shots are bright and clear with good contrast and a sense of action. Deborah Gilmour Smyth and Rick Meads in *Festival of Christmas*, 1987.

Tips for Strong Publicity Photos:

1. The most important element is content. Use action shots that tell a story. These are far superior to static photos of posed people standing or sitting around. To avoid the posed look during a session, have the actors say lines and improvise.

2. Set up a photo shoot for each production. This may take place during rehearsal or at a time determined by the photographer.

3. A simple but dramatic shot of one actor has great impact when used as a large dominant theme on a page. It immediately grabs the emotion of the viewer.

4. Make the background as uncluttered as possible. In printed publicity, this helps a photo to leap off of the page.

5. A light background usually works best with comedy, while a dark background or one with heavy shadows will look dramatic or mysterious.

6. To keep the viewer's eye moving, keep the faces in the photos facing *into* the page.

Guidelines for Press Photos:

1. Keep up-to-date records on each publication, listing address, phone number, and the name of the person to receive the photos. List the photo deadline for monthly periodicals.

2. Make sure your photos are clean, in focus, and with good contrast. You can have quantities of black-and-white, five-by-seven prints made up at a local photo lab. Shop around for the best price.

3. Never use more than three people in a photo. Fewer subjects make for stronger newspaper photos.

4. Have at least one woman in any photo. For some reason it is more likely to be printed.

5. Always attach a label on the back of each photo which lists:

- name of the show
- where and when it is performed
- actors in the photo from left to right
- name of the photographer
- your group's logo, with address, and phone number

Color

Color? That's right. Sure, you have a limited budget, but the experts agree that you need only add one color to your basic black ink to increase readership by at least 50 percent. And one color (as opposed to four color or full color) does not cost that much more. Used with care, an added color can be an interesting spice. With proper use, color attracts attention, emphasizes quality, and sells the message.

Different colors evoke varying responses. After more than a hundred thousand color tests around the world it has been shown that there are universal reactions to color. Here are some of the results of that test:

Blue	—contemplation, peace, contentment, tranquility
Red	—vitality, action, excitement, passion
Green	—assertiveness, tension, self-control, perseverance
Yellow	—optimism, aspiration, expansion, originality
Violet	—enchantment, fantasy
Brown	—security, physical comfort, roots, sensual ease

Black —renunciation, mystery, dignity, high status

Grey —neutral, free of stimulus (however, when combined with black, it provides interest and is an effective highlight)

In a two-color brochure, black-and-white photos generally make the stronger impact (as opposed to another color and white). Stay with white, off-white, or the lighter shades in your choice of paper stock. Readability is paramount, and, almost always, the lighter paper will give you the best results.

Cost Control

- *Screening down* maximizes the use of color. For example, a 20 percent screen of brown appears tan. You're only paying a minimal cost for the screen rather than 40 percent more for a completely different color. Your printer or designer will be able to guide you through this process.

- *Size, shape,* and *color* are all critical cost factors. Get to know the standards in these areas. They cost much less than off-sizes, custom shapes, or exotic colors.

- *Proof everything twice.* Make all your corrections before you get to the printer. It costs to make changes after a piece is ready for print.

- *Plan ahead.* A good printer will be accurate in telling you when the job will be done, if you give them the work on time. If you get it to the printer late, or come back with changes after the due date, you'll have to pay a double rush charge to get it out on time—if they can even do it that fast.

- *Select a cost-effective printer and designer* who will advise you on ways to save money. When they're on your side, you have a great relationship.

Paper costs can vary immensely. A printer's house brand is usually cheaper than the custom sheet you found in a paper-sample catalogue. Ask the printer for a cost on several different kinds of paper. However, do not sacrifice weight of paper for economy. A flimsy-weight paper may cost a little less but will come across to the reader as cheap as well. If you are marketing something, spend the money for quality. If you are just printing to inform, go the economy route.

Personal Communication

Personal communication is the most powerful, yet least expensive form of publicity you can have. It takes many forms:

- Speaking about your drama group to other church and community groups

- One-on-one conversations about your group with the religious, political, and cultural leaders of your community

- Phone conversations with potential sponsors of your traveling productions

- The word of mouth advertising by those who have seen your performances

It is the combined impact of exposure in different media, quality promotional materials, and positive personal communication that will make your marketing a success. But to keep it successful you will need to support these efforts with high-quality dramatic productions.

Most of this chapter has dealt with publicity—grabbing people's attention, telling them who you are, and getting them out to see you. But public relations is much more than publicity. It is every detail of your contact with the public, whether it is answering the office phone, the casual conversation at the supermarket, or greeting patrons at the box-office window. Look for ways to make these contacts pleasant, courteous, and memorable.

You'll have success in public relations when everyone in your group:

- Communicates clearly the group's purpose
- Looks for ways to improve that communication
- Truly cares about the audience

A strong marketing plan and an understanding of the principles we've outlined here will make all the hard work in rehearsals worthwhile. By holding to high standards of quality and integrity in everything from your concept and your conversation to the completed project, you make positive statements about who you are and the God you serve.

12
A Wider View

Archaeologists have uncovered no early stages of human existence so primitive that they were without art. Even before the dawn of civilization we had received this gift from Hands we were not quick enough to discern . . .

Art warms even an icy and depressed heart, opening it to lofty spiritual experience. By means of art we are sometimes sent revelations unattainable by reason. Like that little mirror in the fairy tales—look into it, and you will see not yourself but, for a moment, that which passeth understanding, a realm to which no man can ride or fly. And for which the soul begins to ache . . .

—Aleksandr Solzhenitsyn

We have tried in this book to give you some practical ideas and information for building a small drama group. We hope you have found it of value.

But it is also our hope that you will see the arts as more than just another utilitarian tool for your church program—more than a way to increase attendance, and more than something to hold people's attention until you get to the "important stuff."

The arts are an amazing and significant gift of God. They hold the potential for powerful affirmation or challenge. They can carry their audience to sorrow or delight. They can teach, question, celebrate, and heal.

We live in a culture increasingly concerned with efficiency and the bottom line. We are more interested in "does it work?" than "is it right?" We are quicker to ask "will it sell?" than "is it true?" Science and technology pull us toward a mechanistic view of life. Everything must be "useful." The human heart is lost behind the business plan.

Rather than giving us more leisure time or time for reflection, technology has steadily increased the pace of our lives and raised our level of materialistic expectations. We work more than ever. Spiritual contemplation, individual creativity, and family celebration are all trampled in the rush to serve the modern gods of efficiency and acquisition.

But God has presented us with a balance. We have the gift of Art. It stops us. It reminds us of who we are. It reflects the joy and the pain of our humanness. It refocuses our senses and refreshes our spirits. It points us to the Beautiful and it holds up the Truth. In all of this, it helps us praise and worship the Giver. It reminds us that, as Victor Hugo once remarked, "the beautiful is as useful as the useful."

At Lamb's Players, while we celebrate our calling to serve our imaginative Creator in the arts, we choose not to use the terms *Christian drama* and *Christian theater*. We avoid these terms because: (1) They're confusing. Is *Christian drama* drama meant only *for* Christians? Or is it drama *by* Christians, no matter what the content? Is it evangelistic or didactic? Does it only deal with "Christian" themes? Some people may call a drama that deals with religious subject matter Christian drama. It becomes a matter of semantics, but we see that simply as a thematic category which we would refer to as *religious drama.* To paraphrase C. S. Lewis, Christian drama can exist only in the same sense that Christian cooking exists. What is Christian cooking? Christianity is not a sauce that we can spoon out and ladle over things to make them "okay." But, as Jesus illustrated, it is like the leaven in the loaf. It is not something we put on, rather it fills the whole of who we are. Let us infuse our art with our faith, because it is who we are, not because we are intent on doing the right "Christian" things.

(2) Christian drama connotes second-rate. It's unfortunate, but true. Maybe it shouldn't, but it does. We can easily hide behind antiquated art forms, doing only what is safe and familiar. "And besides," we often hear, "the only thing that really matters is the message." We need to rouse from our artistic slumber. Marshall McLuhan's maxim is true, the medium *is* the message. Form communicates just as strongly as content. Our standards need to be set high for both. Taking poor work and sticking a "Christian" label on it does nothing to either serve Christ or make the work better! As Elton Trueblood said, "Holy shoddy is still shoddy." Our work needs to be truthful, vibrant, fresh, and excellent. It needs to address the hope, the pain, and the joy of people today. And its quality should be a proper reflection of our great Creator!

(3) "Christian" is not something we *do*, it is someone we *are*. In the New Testament, *Christian* refers to a person; it is not a qualification. Only in the recent decades of the last two thousand years has the word *Christian* been used so freely as an adjective; prior to this it was used, almost exclusively, as a noun. But as our culture moved further away from its roots in Christianity, it began to use *Christian* as a qualification.

Ironically, today the church's use of *Christian* as an adjective often keeps us from being salt and light in our culture. It keep us locked in our own basement where we spend all our time talking to ourselves. It becomes easy to spend our time "entertaining the saints," rather than addressing the surrounding culture. We are called to be *in* the world, but not *of* it!

As Christians working in the dramatic arts we have the opportunity to explore all of the concerns and issues of life, under the overarching Lordship of Christ. To reclaim a voice in the dramatic arts we need to pray *and* study, discuss *and* practice. We need to collaborate and to push each other to do our best work. As a church we need to nurture our artists, both amateur and professional. They need our prayer, our encouragement, and our patronage.

*****

> Oh God, whom saints and angels delight to worship in heaven: Be ever present with your servants who seek through the arts to perfect the praises offered by your people on earth; and grant to them even now glimpses of your beauty, and make them worthy at length to behold it unveiled for evermore; through Jesus Christ our Lord. Amen.
>
> —The Book of Common Prayer

Resources

What follows is a series of lists—sources for obtaining copies of plays and scripts; theater associations and support groups; professional theater companies that hold to a Christian world view; and books that will offer more in-depth information on developing a drama group.

While the books are, for the most part, published in the US, we have tried to include information from Canada and Great Britain as well. These lists are by no means exhaustive, but we hope you will find them helpful. If you are aware of any resources you think should be included in this list please send them to:

RESOURCE LIST
c/o Lamb's Players
PO Box 26
National City, CA 92050

Appendix A
Script Sources

These sources range from small performing groups offering photocopies of their scripts, to large professional publishing agencies. Request a catalogue or information on the material they offer. Be clear if you have specific thematic interests or if you are looking for certain theatrical forms (i.e., street theater, children's theater, readers theater, sketches, full-length plays). Be aware of any performance agreements or royalty requirements. Happy hunting!

AD Players
    2710 West Alabama, Houston, TX 77098

Abingdon Press
    201 Eighth Ave., Nashville, TN 37202

Agape Drama
    Box 1313, Englewood, CO 80123

Aldersgate Productions
    12 Palace Street, London SW1E 5JF, England

Augsburg Publishing
    426 S. Fifth St., Minneapolis, MN 55440

Baker Book House
2768 E. Paris Ave., Grand Rapids MI 49546

Baker's Plays
100 Chauncy Street, Boston, MA 02111

Bethany Press
Box 179, St. Louis, MO 63166

Broadman Press
127 Ninth Ave. N., Nashville, TN 37234

Christian Board of Publication
PO Box 179, St. Louis, MO 63166

Collins Liturgical Publications
8 Grafton Street, London W1X 3LA, England

Contemporary Drama Service
PO Box 7710, Colorado Springs, CO 80933

Continental Ministries
PO Box 1996, Thousand Oaks, CA 91360

Dramatic Publishing
PO Box 109, Woodstock, IL 60098

Dramatists Play Service
440 Park Ave. S., New York, NY 10016

Friendship Press
PO Box 37844, Cincinnati, OH 45237

Horizon Gate Productions
PO Box 1740, La Mesa, CA 92041

I. E. Clark
PO Box 246, Schulenburg, TX 78956

Judson Press
Valley Forge, PA 19481

Kingdom Players
PO Box 371289, Decatur, GA 30037

Lamb's Players
PO Box 26, National City, CA 92050

Lillenas Publishing
Box 527, Kansas City, MO 64141

Modern Liturgy
160 E. Virginia St., #290, San Jose, CA 95112

Music Theatre International
49 East 52d St., New York, NY 10022

On Stage
PO Box 25365, Chicago, IL 60625

Pioneer Drama Service
PO Box 22555, Denver, CO 80222

RADIUS (The Religious Drama Society of Great Britain)
St. Paul's Church, Covent Garden, London WC2E 9ED, England.

Riding Lights Theatre
39 Micklegate, York Y01 1JH, England

Russell House
1591 Pioneer Way, El Cajon, CA 92020

Samuel French
45 West Twenty-fifth St., New York, NY 10010
or
7623 Sunset Blvd., Hollywood, CA 90046

Tams-Witmark Music Library
560 Lexington Ave., New York, NY 10022

World Wide Publications
1503 Hennepin Ave., Minneapolis, MN 55403

Appendix B
Associations and Support Groups

Arts Center Group
21 Short Street, London SE1 8LJ, England

CAN (Christians in the Arts Networking)
PO Box 1941, Cambridge, MA 02238

CHART (Chicago Arts Group)
1211 W. Elmdale #2H, Chicago, IL 60660

Christians in Technical Service
7601 Forest City Road, Orlando, FL 32810

CITA (Christians in Theatre Arts)
Malone College, Canton, OH 44709

Charity Technical Support Ministries
1471 Colgate Dr., St. Charles, MO 63303

FACE (Fellowship of Artists for Cultural Evangelism)
1605 E. Elizabeth St., Pasadena, CA 91104

Genesis Arts Trust
21 Short St., London SE1 8LJ, England

LA Arts Group
PO Box 1602, Beverly Hills, CA 90213

New York Arts Group
PO Box 489, Old Chelsea Station, New York, NY 10011

RADIUS (The Religious Drama Society of Great Britain)
St. Paul's Church, Covent Garden, London WC2E 9ED, England.

Schuyler Creative Arts Institute
PO Box 790, San Carlos, CA 94070

Washington Arts Group
2013 "Q" Street NW, Washington, DC 20009

Appendix C
Professional Theater Companies

What follows is a list of touring companies and resident theaters operated by Christians. We do not pretend that the list is complete. We tried to include all the companies we were aware of that consisted of more than one individual, had some full-time staff, and paid their performers. The level of experience, the purpose of the organization, and the quality of productions may vary widely from group to group.

AD Players
2710 W. Alabama, Houston, TX 77098

Acacia Theatre Company
3822 N. Farwell Ave., Shorewood, WI 53211

Brookstone Theatre Company
55 Gage Ave., Toronto, ONT M1J 1T7, Canada

Christian Arts, Inc.
1755 West End Ave., New Hyde Park, NY 11040

City Light Performing Arts
2439 Fifteenth Ave., San Francisco, CA 94116

Covenant Players
PO Box 2900, Oxnard, CA 93033

Footprints
St. Nicholas Rectory, Nottingham NG1 6AE, England

Fountain Square Fools
607 Sycamore Street, Cincinnati, OH 45202

Friends of the Groom
83 Gatch Street, Milford, OH 45150

Iowa Christian Theater
PO Box 322, Washington, IA 52353

Jeremiah People
PO Box 1996, Thousand Oaks, CA 91360

Lamb's Players Theatre
PO Box 26, National City, CA 92050

Lamb's Theatre
130 W. 44th St., New York, NY 10036

Maranatha Productions
PO Box 210, Dixon, IL 61021

Master Arts Company
PO Box 9336, Grand Rapids, MI 49509

Orlando Theatre Project
1005 La Quinta Dr., Orlando, FL 32809

Pacific Theatre
5375 University Blvd., Vancouver, BC V6T 1K3, Canada

The Refreshment Committee
801 Dayton Ave., St. Paul, MN 55104

Riding Lights
39 Micklegate, York YO1 1JH, England

Saltworks Theatre Company
The Design Center, 5001 Baum Boulevard, Pittsburgh, PA 15213

Taproot Theatre Company
PO Box 31116, Seattle, WA 98103

Theatre Roundabout
859 Finchley Road, London NW11 8LX, England

Trinity Theatre
525 Adelaide St. East, Toronto, ONT M5A 4W4, Canada

Westminster Theatre
Palace Street, London SW1E 5JB, England

Youth With a Mission Theatre
PO Box 1324, Cambridge, ONT N1R 7G6, Canada

Appendix D
Press Copy

Press Release and Public Service Announcement

LAMB'S PLAYERS THEATRE

May 8, 1988

Contact: Christian Turner
(619) 474-3385

WORLD PREMIERE TALE OF WONDER OPENS AT LAMB'S PLAYERS!

The World Premiere stage adaptation of **The Book of the Dun Cow** opens on June 24 and will run through July 24 at Lamb's Players Theatre. This fantasy adventure was written by Walter Wangerin, Jr. and heralded "Best Book Of The Year" by the New York Times in 1978.

Robert Smyth and Kerry Meads have teamed up for the challenge of bringing **The Book of the Dun Cow** to the stage. "The heroes of the story are barnyard animals," says Smyth, "but this is not your average children's tale. It is an fascinating look at ultimate evil surprisingly conquered by the faith and courage of frail creatures."

The Book of the Dun Cow is directed by Robert Smyth who has assembled the talents of David Thayer (Light Design), Christian Turner (Set Design), Veronica Murphy Smith and Mike Buckley (Costume Design), and Pamela Turner (Choreographer) for the production.

The Dun Cow and her ensemble of roosters, mice, weasels, etc., will be performed by: Mike Buckley, David Cochran Heath, Kerry Meads, Cynthia Peters, Veronica Murphy Smith, Tom Stephenson, Deborah Gilmour Smyth, Pamela Turner, and Ken Wagner.

The Book of the Dun Cow premieres on June 24 and runs through July 24. Days of performance are Wednesday - Saturday evenings a 8:00 p.m., as well as Saturday and Sunday matinees at 2:00 p.m. Ticket prices are $13 and $15 with discounts available for groups, senior citizens, youth and active military. Tickets may be reserved by calling 474-4542. The box office hours are from 9-5 weekdays and Wednesday - Saturday evenings from 6:30 - 9:30.

###

500 PLAZA BLVD. P.O. BOX 26 NATIONAL CITY CA 92050 • ADMIN.: (619) 474-3385

30 SECOND PSA (55 words)

The mighty, fantasy adventure, **The Book of the Dun Cow** by Walter Wangerin, Jr., opens at Lamb's Players Theatre on Friday, June 24. Performances are Wednesdays through Saturdays at 8 pm, with Saturday and Sunday matinees at 2 pm. **The Book of the Dun Cow** runs through Sunday, July 24. For ticket information call 474-4542.

15 SECOND PSA (33 words)

Lamb's Players Theatre will open the World Premiere Adaptation of **The Book of the Dun Cow** on Friday, June 24. This mighty, fantasy adventure will run through July 24. For ticket information call 474-4542.

ROBERT SMYTH, PRODUCING ARTISTIC DIRECTOR

500 PLAZA BLVD. P.O. BOX 26 NATIONAL CITY CA 92050 • ADMIN.: (619) 474-3385

Further Reading

Acting

Berry, Cicely. *The Actor and His Text.* London: Harrap, 1987.

_____. *Voice and the Actor.* New York: Macmillan, 1973.

Blunt, Jerry. *Stage Dialects.* New York: Harper and Row, 1967.

Callow, Simon. *Being An Actor.* New York: Grove Press, 1988

Chekhov, Michael. *To the Actor.* New York: Harper and Row, 1953.

Cole, T., and H. K. Chinoy, eds. *Actors on Acting.* New York: Crown, 1970.

Glenn, Stanley L. *The Complete Actor.* Boston: Allyn and Bacon, 1977.

Hagen, Uta. *Respect for Acting.* New York: Macmillan, 1973.

Hodgson, J., and E. Richards. *Improvisation.* New York: Grove, 1974.

Johnstone, Keith. *Impro.* New York: Theatre Arts Books, 1979.

Richardson, Don. *Acting Without Agony.* Boston: Allyn and Bacon, 1988.

Shurtleff, Michael. *Audition.* New York: Walker, 1978.

Spolin, Viola. *Improvisation for the Theater.* Evanston, Ill.: Northwestern University Press, 1963.

Suzuki, Tadashi. *The Way of Acting.* New York: Theatre Communications Group, 1986.

Christianity and the Arts

Forbes, Cheryl. *Imagination.* Portland: Multnomah, 1986.

Gaebelein, Frank. *The Christian, the Arts, and Truth.* Portland: Multnomah, 1987.

L'Engle, Madeleine. *Walking on Water.* Wheaton, Ill.: Harold Shaw, 1980.

Rookmaaker, H. R. *The Creative Gift.* Westchester: Cornerstone Books, 1981.

Ryken, Leland. *Culture in Christian Perspective.* Portland: Multnomah, 1987.

Schaeffer, Francis A. *Art and the Bible.* Downers Grove, Ill.: InterVarsity, 1973.

Schaeffer, Franky. *Addicted to Mediocrity.* Westchester: Crossway Books, 1981.

Veith, Gene Edward. *The Gift of Art.* Downers Grove, Ill.: InterVarsity, 1983.

Watts, Murray. *Christianity and the Theatre.* Edinburgh, Scotland: Handsel Press, 1986.

Whittle, Donald. *Christianity and the Arts.* Philadelphia: Fortress, 1966.

Wolterstorff, Nicholas. *Art in Action.* Grand Rapids, Mich.: Wm. B. Eerdmans, 1980.

Costumes

Arnold, Janet. *Patterns of Fashion,* vol. 1 *1660–1860;* vol. 2 *1860–1940.* New York: Drama Book Specialists, 1977.

Covey, E. and R. Ingham. *The Costumer's Handbook.* Englewood Cliffs, N.J.: Prentice Hall, 1980.

Laver, James. *A Concise History of Costumes and Fashion.* New York: Harry N. Abrams, 1969.

Motley, A. *Designing and Making Stage Costumes.* New York: Watson-Guptill, 1964.

Waugh, Nora. *The Cut of Men's Clothes, 1600–1900.* New York: Theatre Arts Books, 1964.

———.*The Cut of Women's Clothes, 1600-1930.* New York: Theatre Arts Books, 1968.

Wilcox, R. Turner. *The Mode in Costume.* New York: Scribner, 1958.

Directing

Ball, William. *A Sense of Direction.* New York: Drama Book Publishers, 1984.

Clurman, Harold. *On Directing.* New York: Macmillan, 1972.

Cole, T., and H. K. Chinoy, eds. *Directors on Directing.* New York: Crown Publishers, 1970.

Carra, L., and A. Dean. *Fundamentals of Play Directing.* New York: Holt, Rinehart, and Winston, 1965.

Spolin, Viola. *Theater Games for Rehearsal: A Director's Handbook.* Evanston, Ill.: Northwestern University Press, 1985.

Drama Ideas for the Church

Bennett, Gordon. *Readers Theater Comes to Church.* Colorado Springs: Meriwether Publishing, 1987.

Burbridge, Paul, and Murray Watts. *Time to Act.* Downers Grove: InterVarsity Press, 1979.

Duckworth, Liz and John. *The No-Frills Guide to Youth Group Drama.* Wheaton, Ill.: Victor Books, 1985.

Johnson, Albert. *Church Plays and How to Stage Them.* Philadelphia: United Church Press, 1966.

Johnson, Beverly. *Drama in the Church.* Minneapolis: Augsburg Publishing, 1983.

Lewis, Todd. *A Readers Theater Ministry.* Kansas City: Lillenas Publishing, 1988.

Litherland, Janet. *Getting Started in Drama Ministry*. Colorado Springs: Meriwether Publishing, 1988.

Read, S., and W. Fry. *Christian Theatre*. London: Eyre and Spottiswoode, 1986.

Waddy, Lawrence. *Drama in Worship*. New York: Paulist Press, 1978.

Management

Horwitz, Tem. *Arts Administration*. Chicago: Chicago Review Press, 1978.

Langley, Stephen. *Theatre Management in America*. New York: Drama Book Specialists, 1974.

Shagan, Rena. *The Road Show*. New York: American Council for the Arts, 1985.

Wolf, Thomas. *The Nonprofit Organization*. New Jersey: Prentice-Hall, 1984.

Marketing

Bayan, Richard. *Words That Sell*. Brentwood: Asher-Gallant Press, 1987.

Gedney, K., and P. Fultz *The Complete Guide to Creating Successful Brochures*. Brentwood: Asher-Gallant Press, 1986.

Melillo, Joseph, ed. *Market the Arts!* New York: FEDAPT, 1983.

Morison, B. G., and J. G. Dalgleish. *Waiting in the Wings.* New York: American Council for the Arts, 1987.

Newman, Danny. *Subscribe Now!* New York: Theatre Communications Group, 1981.

Graphics

Laundy, P., and M. Vignelli. *Graphic Design for the Nonprofit Organization.* New York: American Institute of Graphic Arts.

Skal, David, ed. *Graphic Communications for the Performing Arts.* New York: Theatre Communications Group, 1981.

White, Jan. *Graphic Ideas Notebook.* Cincinnati: Watson-Guptill Publications, 1984.

Technical

Bellman, Willard. *Lighting the Stage.* New York: Harper and Row, 1967.

Corson, Richard. *Stage Make-Up.* New Jersey: Prentice-Hall, 1981.

Parker, W. O., and H. K. Smith. *Scene Design and Stage Lighting.* New York: Holt, Rinehart, and Winston, 1979.

Pecktal, Lynn. *Designing and Painting for the Theatre.* New York: Holt, Rinehart, and Winston, 1982.

Streader, Tim and John Williams. *Create Your Own Stage Lighting.* New Jersey: Prentice-Hall, 1985.

Thomas, Terry. *Create Your Own Stage Sets.* New Jersey: Prentice-Hall, 1985

Welker, David. *Stagecraft.* Boston: Allyn and Bacon, 1987.

Theater

Brook, Peter. *The Empty Space.* New York: Atheneum, 1981.

Grotowski, Jerzy. *Towards a Poor Theatre.* New York: Simon and Schuster, 1968.

London, Todd. *The Artistic Home.* New York: Theatre Communications Group, 1988.

Writing

Catron, Louis E. *Writing, Producing, and Selling Your Play.* New Jersey: Prentice-Hall, 1984.

Gardner, John. *On Moral Fiction.* New York: Basic Books, 1978.

Grebanier, Bernard. *Playwriting.* New York: Harper and Row, 1979.

Korty, Carol. *Writing Your Own Plays: Creating, Adapting, Improvising.* New York: Scribner & Sons, 1986.

Contributors

Contributors to *Developing a Drama Group* are all part of Lamb's Players, a professional theater company based in San Diego, California. The company maintains a full-time ensemble of actors, designers, directors, and playwrights exploring the integration of the Christian faith with the demands of the professional theater. Lamb's Players Theatre, the company's resident stage, opened in 1978 and now operates a year-round production schedule. Along with fresh productions of the classics and the discovery of lesser-known works, the troupe is committed to the development of new work by playwrights writing from a broad-based Christian world view. Since its founding in 1971, Lamb's Players Touring Companies have performed across the country and internationally to well over a million people on college campuses, military bases and beaches, in churches, convention centers, prisons, and parks.

The book is the product of the combined and generous efforts of many people. For these we wish to offer our heartfelt thanks.

A special thanks goes out to Lamb's Players staff members, Nathan Peirson (photography); Dave and Beth Heath (proofreading); Ruth Lacy (typing and correspondence); and to the people who took time out from their already hectic schedules to set pen to paper and so graciously share their theatrical expertise with fellow enthusiasts of the stage. They are:

Robert Smyth (chapters 1, 2, 3, 4, 6, and 12), the Producing Artistic Director of Lamb's Players. He has been with Lamb's Players since 1976 and now oversees the company's overall work. His hats include those of administrator, director, playwright, and occasional performer. He has directed over forty productions and written or co-written several plays including adaptations of Bram Stoker's *Dracula* and Walter Wangerin's *The Book of the Dun Cow*, and the musical *Journey* with composer James Ward. His credits as a performer include a critically acclaimed one-man performance on the life of the leper priest Damien de Veuster. In addition to his work at the Theatre, Robert is an active speaker and seminar leader and is on the faculty of the Julian Study Center.

Kerry Meads (chapter 5), is an Associate Director of Lamb's Players. As the company's resident playwright, she has produced six world premieres including Lamb's Players annual *Festival of Christmas.* She has co-authored acclaimed adaptations of *Dracula* and *The Book of the Dun Cow.* Her original work for Lamb's Players Touring Companies has been published and performed internationally. Kerry is also a director and actor with the Theatre's resident ensemble.

Deborah Gilmour Smyth (chapter 7), has been a member of Lamb's Players Theatre's resident ensemble since 1979. Recognized as one of San Diego's leading actors, her long list of credits includes acclaimed performances as Joan in *Saint Joan*, Kate in *Taming of the Shrew*, Tatania in *A Midsummer Night's Dream*, Anita in *West Side Story* and Anne Sullivan in *The Miracle Worker.* Her background in musical theater included work at San Francisco State and SRT in Santa Rosa before coming to Lamb's Players. An accomplished singer and dancer, as an Associate Director with the Theatre she also directs on occasion.

Veronica Murphy Smith (chapter 8), graduated from California State University, San Bernadino and was a costumer at the Boarshead Theatre in Lansing Michigan before coming to Lamb's Players Theatre in 1985. As Costume Supervisor/Designer, she oversees the production schedules for the resident stage as well as numerous touring productions. She has designed costumes for more than twenty productions at Lamb's Players including *Amadeus, Much Ado About Nothing, Joseph and the Amazing Technicolor Dreamcoat*, and *Saint Joan*. Vicki is also a design consultant and actor.

Mike Buckley (chapters 9 and 10), joined Lamb's Players in 1984, after receiving his M.F.A. in Scenic Design from U.C.L.A. and teaching technical theater at Biola University. His designs have been seen by thousands of theatergoers and he continues to receive praise for their originality. Among his credits are sets for *Talley's Folly, Rhinoceros, The Miser, 1776, The Foreigner, Amadeus, An Inspector Calls*, and *The Diary of Anne Frank*. Mike also works as a design consultant, playwright, and occasional actor.

Christian Turner (chapter 11), was a member of Lamb's Players' first full-time Street Theatre Troupe in 1972. He worked as a performer and director with the Lamb's Players puppet troupe, Quimby Co. He now puts his graphic arts skills to good use as Lamb's Players' Art Director, overseeing all marketing and graphic design. He has designed sets for the Resident Theatre and can occasionally be seen as a performer. Chris also works as a freelance consultant and designer for a wide variety of organizations.